W9-BJS-636

ROCKFORD PUBLIC LIBRARY
3 1112 01603931 1

WITHDRAWN

GREAT HISTORIC DISASTERS

HURRICANE KATRINA

GREAT HISTORIC DISASTERS

The Atomic Bombings of Hiroshima and Nagasaki

The Black Death

The Dust Bowl

The Great Chicago Fire of 1871

The *Hindenburg* Disaster of 1937

Hurricane Katrina

The Indian Ocean Tsunami of 2004

The Influenza Pandemic of 1918–1919

The Johnstown Flood of 1889

The San Francisco Earthquake and Fire of 1906

The Sinking of the *Titanic*

The Triangle Shirtwaist Factory Fire

GREAT HISTORIC DISASTERS

HURRICANE KATRINA

JAMIE PIETRAS

HURRICANE KATRINA

Chelsea House
An imprint of Infobase Publishing
132 West 31st Street
New York NY 10001

Library of Congress Cataloging-in-Publication Data
Pietras, Jamie.
Hurricane Katrina/Jamie Pietras.
p. cm.—(Great historic disasters)
Includes bibliographical references and index.
ISBN: 978-0-7910-9639-0 (hardcover)
1. Hurricane Katrina, 2005. 2. Hurricanes—Louisiana—New Orleans. 3. Disaster victims—Louisiana—New Orleans. 4. Disaster relief—Louisiana— New Orleans. I. Title. II. Series.
HV636 2005 .L8 P54 2008
976'.044—dc22 2007036551

Chelsea House books are available at special discounts when purchased in bulk quantities for businesses, associations, institutions, or sales promotions. Please call our Special Sales Department in New York at (212) 967-8800 or (800) 322-8755.

You can find Chelsea House on the World Wide Web at http://www.chelseahouse.com

Text design by Annie O'Donnell
Cover design by Ben Peterson

Printed in the United States of America

Bang KT 10 9 8 7 6 5 4 3 2 1

This book is printed on acid-free paper.

All links and Web addresses were checked and verified to be correct at the time of publication. Because of the dynamic nature of the Web, some addresses and links may have changed since publication and may no longer be valid.

Contents

Introduction: The "Big Easy" in Crisis

When the first signs of sunlight peeked through the trickling rain the morning of Monday August 29, 2005, many residents of the city of New Orleans hoped the worst was behind them. Hours earlier, the tropical hurricane known as Katrina had blown through the night sky, making landfall at an area just 70 miles to the southeast of the city and tearing the roofs off of buildings and tossing boats like they were confetti. Millions in the Gulf States of Mississippi, Louisiana, and Alabama were left without power and transportation thanks to ferocious winds that extended beyond the eye of the storm and some initial flooding that submerged highways. At least 35 people were dead, according to later news reports. Shining warmly, the sun seemed to be offering a gesture of peace, the first in days.

Despite nature's reconciliation, others in the balmy, wind-torn city knew they could not completely relax. City and state leaders wondered whether the city's levees—artificial, earthen barriers designed to protect it from lake and river floodwaters—would hold up as intended. The levees were old, fragile, and poorly designed. If they wore away during a storm, millions of gallons of water could pass over them and spew into the streets. Though thousands of residents emerged without a scratch from the storm's relentless beating, they understood its secondary dangers. A failure of the levees meant that homes, cars, and even people could be swept up in severe, all-consuming floodwaters. The city would fill up like an aquarium.

Living in a boarding home in a particularly flood-prone neighborhood known as the Lower Ninth Ward, 56-year-old Frank Mills had less than a few hours of wishful thinking. Around 8:15 A.M., murky, brown water began filling his living room, rising steadily toward the ceiling. According to reports from the Associated Press, Mills was sharing the house with three elderly residents, each of whom quickly scampered

Hurricane Katrina caused millions of dollars in damage in Louisiana, Mississippi, and Alabama in 2005. Photos of New Orleans under water, such as this one, showed only part of the storm's aftermath.

upstairs. One of the men realized he had left something in his bedroom and went with a female resident to retrieve it. When Mills saw the woman next, she was floating face up in the hallway. He never saw the man again.

Mills climbed onto a roof overlooking the front porch. He watched as the floodwater slapped relentlessly against the building. Another resident tried to join him, but could not find the strength to hoist himself over the roof's ledge. His frail fingers loosened their grip, and then he let go completely. All Mills could do was watch as the current swept him away. "I don't know if he drowned or had a heart attack," he recalled somberly. Had it not been for a piece of floating medical equipment, Mills might not have made it out alive either. After waiting for two hours, he hitched a ride on top of the device and paddled his way to a nearby building. "I was next, that's what I was thinking," he told the AP.

Nervous thoughts filled the heads of thousands of New Orleans residents as they hatched similar escape plans. People blasted holes through their roofs using axes, hammers, and shotguns; they made boats out of refrigerators and other buoyant appliances; and they used plastic storage bins as floating baby strollers. In the face of danger, there was no limit to human ingenuity. Nor was there any limit to the generosity of neighbors living in particularly flooded areas such as the Lakeview, Gentilly, the Lower Ninth Ward, and St. Bernard Parish to the east of the city. Storm survivors became the "first responders" to the disaster situation that followed, helping to save and evacuate fellow residents trapped in their homes, rooftops, and trees. Katrina made heroes of everyday citizens, unsung rescuers who did most of their deeds away from news cameras, conducting rescue operations on canoes and motorboats well into the evening hours.

Still, as the storm let up Monday afternoon and the images from New Orleans dominated the news—entire neighborhoods submerged in water, desperate citizens crying from their rooftops for help, and more solemnly, corpses floating facedown in what commentators referred to as the "toxic gumbo" that was now New Orleans—it became clear that America was facing its worst disaster since the September 11, 2001, attacks on the World Trade Center and Pentagon. Only this time, the destruction was not the work of terrorists but the inevitable force of nature. The levees had broken—not in one spot, but in several locations along each of the city's major waterways. All afternoon, calls poured in to emergency workers about people trapped inside their homes. The governor of Louisiana spoke to President George W. Bush, pleading that "we need your help. We need everything you've got."

Unfortunately, many in New Orleans did not receive the help they needed. Despite the heroic efforts of organizations such as Louisiana's Department of Wildlife and Fisheries and the U.S. Coast Guard, government agencies at the city, state, and federal level failed to respond to the needs of flood victims. Survivors in need of food, water, and medical attention sat helpless along the city's sweltering highways and in the Superdome and Ernest N. Morial Convention Center, where tens of thousands were left stranded. Worse yet, others remained trapped in their homes. In an attempt to coordinate relief efforts, the Federal Emergency Management Agency (FEMA) implemented strict disaster-response rules that made it difficult for organizations to offer assistance. When hurricane victims needed its help the most, FEMA dragged its feet, waiting five whole days before it sent precious supplies to the convention center.

The disaster was among the worst in United States history, killing more than 1,600 people and destroying 200,000 homes along the Gulf Coast. More than one million people fled the Gulf region, where economic losses and property damages were expected to reach a record $125 billion. When flooding was at its peak, an estimated 80 percent of New Orleans's buildings were completely submerged. Because of its cultural and economic significance, New Orleans is often the focal point in discussions about the disaster. But the storm's damages were widespread and equally devastating in neighboring Mississippi, where Governor Haley Barbour described on CBS's August 31 episode of the *Early Show* "[streets] totally covered with lumber, debris, shingles, furniture, and clothes so that you can't see any asphalt for miles around." The small Mississippi town of Waveland was virtually wiped off the map. "There's nothing left," mourned one resident, returning to the scrap pile that was once his home.

Just as Katrina brought out the best in some citizens, it brought out the worst in others. Taking advantage of weakened police and security forces after the storm, looters tore through commercial retail stores such as Wal-Mart, stealing Xboxes, DVDs, and flat-screen television sets. Scam artists posed as representatives of charitable organizations in the hopes of stealing from donors who thought their money was going to help Katrina victims. The disaster took a disproportionate toll on society's most vulnerable members: the poor, the sick, the disabled, and the elderly. In doing so, it forced Americans to confront difficult issues of poverty, racial and class inequality, and environmental neglect.

Puzzled Americans could only ask questions as they witnessed the desperate pleas of Gulf Coast residents night after night. How could an entire American city fill with water? Why did it take five days for the federal government to respond? While some believed the storm and its furious aftermath to be acts of God, answers to these questions can also be found in the more tangible world of basic human error. They lie partially in the history of New Orleans, where environmental neglect and poor planning helped create a disaster waiting to happen.

1 Gateway to the Mississippi

From a geographical perspective, the choice of New Orleans as the location of a major American city never made much sense. Located on the southeastern tip of Louisiana along the Gulf of Mexico, the city sits an average of six feet below sea level and in some parts as many as 10. Meteorologists often liken it to a giant bowl, bordered by the 630-square-mile Lake Pontchartrain to the north and the Mississippi River to the south. Spanish explorers first trekked through the area in 1543, when it was inhabited by Native Americans, but it would not be for another 140 years that Europeans claimed it for themselves. In 1682, French explorer René-Robert Cavelier, sieur de La Salle declared that all land between the Allegheny and the Rocky Mountains was now the property of France's King Louis XIV.

Before La Salle could turn this undeveloped land into a city, one of his own men shot and killed him. A fellow Frenchman, Jean-Baptiste Le Moyne, sieur de Bienville, picked up where the late La Salle left off in 1718, organizing development of the ground where the Mississippi River pointed toward Lake Pontchartrain. Why such an interest in swampland? After all, few would find snakes, alligators, and the threat of constant flooding appealing. The real draw lay in the region's extensive waterways, which offered great potential for commercial shipping. With easy access to the lake, the river, and the Gulf of Mexico, the undeveloped land could be transformed into an important port city, a commercial hub in the increasingly rich new land then known as America.

In order to make this dream a reality, the French needed strong, durable laborers. So, the king began sending prisoners, bonded servants, and African slaves to the Louisiana Gulf. A French speculator lured fellow countrymen to the area with false promises of gold. When they arrived, they found only slaves, criminals, and angry Native Americans, unhappy about the foreign intrusion upon their land. To

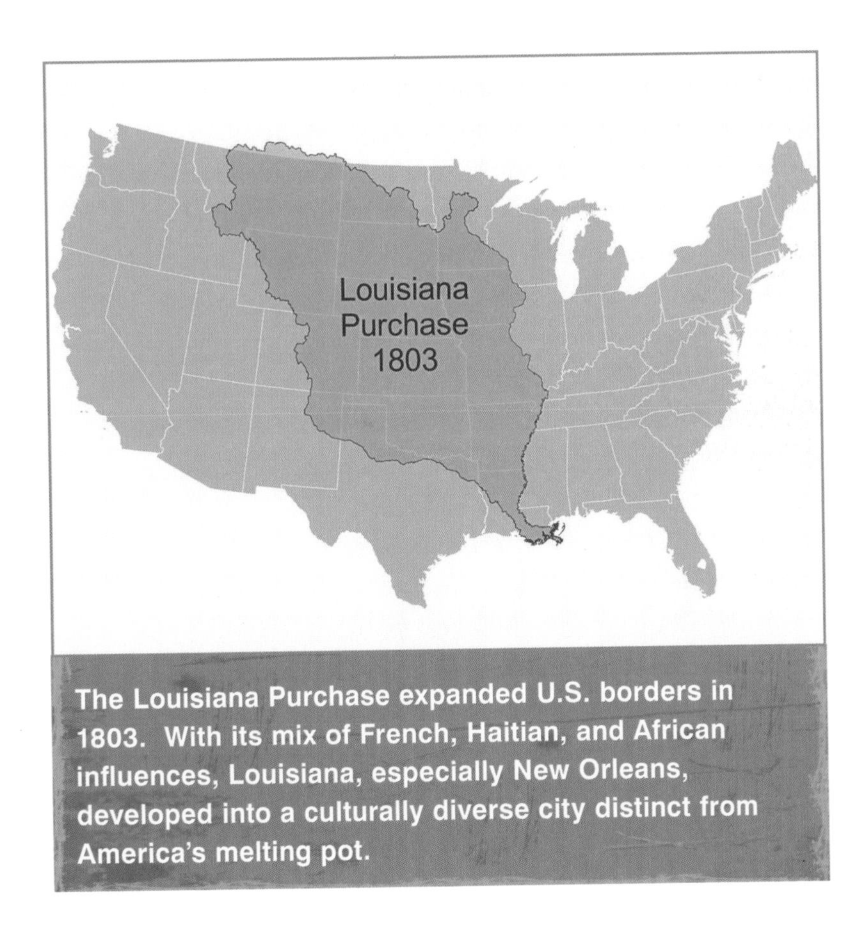

The Louisiana Purchase expanded U.S. borders in 1803. With its mix of French, Haitian, and African influences, Louisiana, especially New Orleans, developed into a culturally diverse city distinct from America's melting pot.

help lift sinking spirits, the French government sent 90 female prisoners to serve as the settlers' "wives." Before New Orleans's notorious "Red Light District" came to symbolize rampant drinking and prostitution, the city was already earning a wild and lawless reputation.

On September 23 and 24, 1722, Mother Nature offered a taste of troubles to come. "The Great Hurricane" ripped through the city, destroying 36 huts, an area hospital, and a church. Floodwaters rose more than eight feet in some areas. Bienville was pressured to move the port settlement further inland, but he stubbornly refused. Moving inland would mean that ships would have had to travel greater distances against the current of the Mississippi River. This navigation was difficult to do using standard sailing equipment. So, rather than move, Bienville decided to instead build stronger levees.

The French turned the city of New Orleans over to the Spanish in 1762 in order to repay a debt. Descendants of early French and Spanish settlers who came to populate large swaths of the city came to identify themselves as *Creoles*. Settling alongside them were French-speaking immigrants from Canada, who were commonly referred to as Cajuns. During the 1790s and early 1800s, a number of newly emancipated Haitian refugees added to the cultural mix, having fled their homeland for Louisiana after successfully revolting against their French colonizers.

BUILDING NEW ORLEANS

Spanish rule of New Orleans was short-lived. France retained control of Louisiana in 1800 and resold it to the United States as part of the historic Louisiana Purchase of 1803. The Louisiana Purchase was a great deal for the Americans, who paid a mere $15 million, roughly four cents for every acre. It doubled the nation's size and gave it control over the Mississippi River as well as the port city.

Though some African Americans enjoyed freedom in New Orleans, enslaved Africans continued to serve as laborers and domestic servants throughout the 1800s. After Congress abolished slavery in 1865, many African Americans remained in the Mississippi Delta region, establishing a musical community responsible for two of the United States's most important cultural innovations: blues and jazz music. Artists such as Louis Armstrong emerged from rough-and-tumble New Orleans neighborhoods and began using music to express the range of their experiences—from mournful blues to happy-go-lucky swing and bebop. Armstrong was known for his ear-to-ear smile and his frenetic, improvised solos. He epitomized

Famous musicians, such as Louis Armstrong and Fats Domino, helped develop blues and jazz music in New Orleans. Places like Preservation Hall in the French Quarter, as seen here in 2004, are dedicated to promoting the music of New Orleans.

the freewheeling world of classical jazz and its derivative forms. Armstrong and later musicians, such as piano star Fats Domino, represented the heart and soul of New Orleans, a multicultural, artist-friendly community.

With its world-class music and cuisine, New Orleans fast became a tourist destination, known for the bars and restaurants that lined its famous "French Quarter." It also developed a reputation for its friendliness and laid-back way of life, which earned the city nicknames such as "The Big Easy" and "The City That Care Forgot." The most well-known New Orleans attraction, the annual Mardi Gras festival, attracted hundreds of thousands of tourists each spring. They flocked to the city for two weeks of parades, parties, and food that highlighted the city's cultural diversity. During Mardi Gras, local chefs served piping hot plates of jambalaya, a French- and Spanish-influenced dish consisting of rice seasoned with shrimp, oysters, ham, or chicken, as well as gumbo, a spicy stew made with meat and okra that can be traced back to West African cooking traditions.

Paying homage to the city in the 1998 sequel to the movie *The Blues Brothers*, the Louisiana Gator Boys echoed a widely held love of New Orleans when they sang:

A come on take a stroll down to Basin Street
Listen to the music with that Dixieland beat
Well the magnolia blossoms fill the air
You ain't been to heaven till you been down there.

Despite its success with tourism, the city failed to attract other types of businesses. Shortly after World War II, however, when engineers determined how to pump oil using offshore rigs stationed in the Gulf, the New Orleans region took on new importance as a source of crude oil. Millions of barrels of oil and trillions of cubic feet of natural gas would be extracted from the region beginning in the 1950s.

ECONOMIC DISPARITY

As the city grew and developed, the threat of flooding remained. After the United States acquired New Orleans

Naming Hurricanes

When a tropical storm develops on the Atlantic Ocean, officials with the World Meteorological Association assign it a name such as "Wilma" or "Katrina." Before 1979, they used female names exclusively, but they eventually changed that policy so that storms are now given male names such as "Alberto" and "Gordon" as well. Naming storms allows meteorologists and public safety officials to keep better track of them, especially when there is more than one storm occurring at a given time. If a storm grows to be strong enough to be classified as a hurricane, it keeps the same name it had as a tropical storm.

Storms in the Atlantic are typically given French-, English-, or Spanish-sounding names, and each begins with a different letter of the 26-letter English alphabet except for the letters Q, U, X, Y, and Z. During any given season, then, the World Meteorological Association is equipped to name just 21 storms. The unusually high number of storms that occurred in 2005 used up the available number of names, so the World Meteorological Association did something it had never done before. It began naming storms after the letters of the Greek alphabet. Therefore, the final tropical storms of the year were called "Alpha," "Beta," "Gamma," "Delta," "Epsilon," and "Zeta."

Known for its music, food, and nightlife, New Orleans became famous for its unique, lively atmosphere. Here, tourists celebrate and catch beads thrown from a parade float during New Orleans's famous Mardi Gras festival.

through the Louisiana Purchase, the federal government began developing a system of revamped levees to prevent lake and river floodwater from flowing into the neighborhoods. It also facilitated the building of canals that pumped water from the city back to Lake Pontchartrain. Those with money generally settled into higher-elevation parts of the city, while the poor settled into low-lying areas such as the Lower Ninth, Treme, and certain sections of New Orleans East.

In New Orleans, stark poverty was always present, though not necessarily visible to the outside world. Rarely did visitors to the French Quarter detour into the Ninth Ward during Mardi Gras, so wealth disparities festered outside of the limelight. As scholar Michael Eric Dyson pointed out in *Come Hell or High Water*, a book on his examination of race and class in the wake of Hurricane Katrina, Mississippi and Louisiana are the two poorest states in the nation. African Americans living in these states earned incomes that were 40 percent less than those earned by whites. Before the storm, New Orleans had a poverty rate of 23 percent, nearly double the national average of 13.1 percent. Roughly 68 percent of its residents had some African heritage.

It was important for city planners to understand poverty, since it played a big role in the public response to a hurricane situation. City leaders could tell people to pack, leave the city, and stay in hotels or with relatives when a destructive storm threatened. Whether residents could actually do so was another matter. Not everyone had friends or relatives with whom they could stay. And hotels cost money. For more than 90,000 Louisiana, Alabama, and Mississippi residents who made less than $10,000 per year, even a one- or two-night hotel expense would not be economically possible. There was also the problem of transportation. About 134,000 New Orleans residents did not own or have access to a car.

While city, state, and federal leaders needed to be aware of the financial resources at residents' disposal, they also needed to be sensitive to the elderly and those with disabilities, as they also had special needs in disaster situations. According to author Dyson, children and the elderly made up 38 percent of New Orleans's population and nearly half of those households were without automobiles. More than 100,000 New Orleans residents were disabled. They included people who were blind or deaf; people who used wheelchairs, walkers, crutches, or service animals; as well as those with mental health needs. Immobile citizens were forced to depend solely on relatives, nurses, boarding room supervisors, or others to whom their well-being was ultimately entrusted.

Unfortunately, during the early morning of April 29, 2005, all the elderly New Orleans residents who remained in their homes, hospitals, or nursing homes could do was pray that someone would be watching out for them. But, as Frank Mills found out, somewhere, somehow, their guardians had failed them.

2 A Sitting Target

Katrina may have been the most famous hurricane of 2005, but it was hardly the only one. A record-setting 15 hurricanes rocked the Atlantic Ocean during the "hurricane season" that occurs from June to November, breaking the previous record of 12, which was set in 1969. The strength of the 2005 storms was cause for even greater alarm. Less than two months after Katrina devastated the Gulf Coast, the most intense hurricane on record roared through Cuba, Mexico, and Florida in October, leaving a trail of 63 casualties and billions of dollars worth of property damage in its wind-torn path. At its peak, Hurricane Wilma registered a record low pressure of 882 millibars (mb) and winds of 185 miles per hour (mph). Like Katrina, Wilma was a Category 5 storm, a classification meteorologists reserve for only the most destructive of hurricanes. Category 5 hurricanes appear, on average, less than once every three years. In 2005, four occurred in a single season.

Hurricane Strength Categories

In 1969, engineer Herbert Saffir and Robert Simpson, the meteorologist in charge of the National Hurricane Center, came up with the idea of categorizing hurricanes based on their wind speeds, the severity of any potential storm surge, and other criteria. Before the men devised their hurricane scale, weather forecasters had no way to communicate the severity of a coming storm to government officials and ordinary citizens. According to the Saffir-Simpson Hurricane scale, storms would be rated on a scale of "categories" from 1 to 5. A Category 1 storm was relatively minor, with winds of 74–95 mph and damage limited only to unanchored mobile homes, shrubs, and trees. Flooding was minor and limited to the coast.

HOW HURRICANES FORM

A hurricane forms when thunderstorms gather together over warm ocean waters. In order for these storms to evolve into a hurricane, four specific weather conditions must occur: low air pressure, warm temperatures, moist ocean air, and tropical winds blowing from near the equator. Low air pressure allows for the formation of a "tropical wave," a large low-pressure air mass which typically begins moving to the west, bringing clouds and rainfall. Next, as warm ocean air rises into the low pressure area, it is replaced by colder air from above. This results in blustering winds as well as increased rain and cloudiness. These conditions indicate the formation of a "tropical disturbance." In as little as 12 hours, or up to two days later, this disturbance can upgrade to a "tropical depression"

A middle-range Category 3 storm, like the one that came down in New Orleans in 1965, could be expected to produce winds of 111–130 mph, causing "some structural damage to small residences and utility buildings" and completely destroying mobile homes. Coastal flooding would destroy smaller structures and even damage larger buildings with floating debris.

A Category 5 storm was the rarest and most catastrophic of all. It could cause "complete roof failure" in most homes and industrial buildings and even blow smaller buildings away. All structures located less than 15 feet above sea level and within 100 yards of the shoreline could expect major damage to their lower floors. The scale's creators recommended the evacuation of residential areas on low ground within 10 miles of the shoreline during such a storm.

as air pressure falls and winds begin to move counterclockwise at speeds of 23–39 mph. Because of the Earth's rotation, the winds blow circularly instead of straight, a phenomenon known as the Coriolis effect.

These winds begin pushing warm, vapor-filled air toward the sky as they reach speeds of 39–73 mph, and then they form the familiar pinwheel pattern typically associated with hurricanes. At this stage, the weather disturbance is called a tropical storm. Usually about 15–20 miles in diameter, the center of a tropical storm is a point of extremely low pressure. A record-setting 27 tropical and subtropical storms occurred in the Atlantic in 2005, and each of them was given a customary storm name so that they could be more easily identified and tracked by the National Hurricane Center in Miami.

Hurricanes develop over warm water and generate torrential rain, high winds, and giant waves, which can cause a great amount of damage. This is a satellite image of Hurricane Wilma, which blew through Cuba, Mexico, and Florida less than two months after Hurricane Katrina devastated the Gulf Coast.

Of all the 2005 storms, none would be as memorable as Katrina, the name assigned to the tropical depression that strengthened off of the coast of Long Island, Bahamas, the morning of Wednesday, August 24. All that anyone living along the Atlantic and Gulf Coasts could do was hope or pray that Katrina would not grow into a full-fledged hurricane.

It is not that tropical storms are not damaging. A tropical storm is actually a serious problem for anything that lies in its path—its wind and rain can knock down trees and power lines and cause mudslides. Officials and weather forecasters living in southeast Florida spent the evening before Katrina's first landfall warning residents to stock up on supplies, board their homes, and get ready for about 20 inches of rain. Still,

Florida residents must have been hoping that Katrina would not become a hurricane before landfall. With winds of 74 to 155-plus mph, hurricanes can shatter windows or even rip the roofs off of people's homes.

REMEMBERING HURRICANE BETSY

Many people think rain is a hurricane's greatest weapon. In fact, a hurricane causes far greater damage with its storm surge, the water it pushes up to shore when it reaches land. The last time New Orleans had to deal with a hurricane and its devastating surge was back on September 9, 1965, when Hurricane Betsy touched down near the mouth of the Mississippi River. The waters of Lake Pontchartrain "sloshed like water in a saucer under the powerful winds," the *Chicago Tribune* reported on September 10. The seven-foot-tall levees along the lake were no match for the 12-foot-surge, which poured over them like a waterfall. Flooding occurred in neighborhoods near the river and lake. Panic-stricken residents helplessly waited out the flood from attics and roofs in the Lower Ninth Ward, Gentilly, and nearby Chalmette in St. Bernard Parish. Waters rose high above car windows and even low-hanging rooftops.

The *Tribune*'s description of the storm's aftermath was eerily similar to scenes it would describe when reporters rushed to cover Katrina 40 years later. First, half of the city's power was knocked out. Then, looters took to the streets of the semi-abandoned city, relishing in the lawlessness and chaos that resulted when police and other emergency response workers had their attention diverted to bigger issues. Returning home after having fled the storm, 100,000 New Orleanians were greeted by the sight of "windows smashed, many homes flattened, roofs peeled off like sardine tins, trees felled, fences splintered," according to the September 11 edition of the *Los Angeles Times*.

After Betsy, the U.S. government realized that stronger levees were needed to protect New Orleans from future flood damage. The responsibility for constructing these levees fell on the U.S. Army Corps of Engineers, a federal organization consisting mostly of civilians who work with military officials to build military bases, dams, and other structures intended to serve the American people. Wherever floodwater from the lake, river, or canals threatened to spill into the Big Easy, the engineers constructed levees and floodwalls that they hoped would be more effective than those which had failed during Betsy.

But even these new and improved structures suffered from fatal design flaws. Everyone in New Orleans had to contend with the unavoidable problem of the soil, which was notoriously moist and provided a weak foundation for construction. An 1849 map of the Lakeview neighborhood illustrates just how bad this land was, as it referred to the area south of the lake and east of the two-mile stretch of the 17th Street Canal as "Swamp Forest."

This is where army engineers overestimated the strength of soil and thus failed to drive the sheet piles that anchored the levees far enough underground. When Katrina's floodwaters finally came rushing through, they actually seeped *underneath* the levees. In other cases, the engineers built floodwalls that were so tall they were unstable and ended up shifting under the weight of the storm.

The Corps made another critical engineering mistake by failing to take into account the impact that the Mississippi River Gulf Outlet (MRGO) would have on hurricane intensity. Constructed in 1965, the 76-mile-long, 36-foot-deep canal was designed to provide a shortcut between the Gulf of Mexico and New Orleans's inner harbor. But it unintentionally magnified hurricane strength. Basically, it acted like a "funnel" straight to New Orleans, raising storm surges by as much as three feet and increasing their velocity.

The flood-prevention system should have been built to withstand a relatively moderate Category 3 storm. When Katrina finally came to Louisiana, that is exactly what it was—a Category 3. Unfortunately, it was also the first major test of New Orleans's revamped flood-prevention network, and it "just overwhelmed the system" according to Stevan

Because New Orleans is below sea level and sandwiched by two bodies of water, flooding in the city was inevitable. Lake Pontchartrain, seen at the top of the satellite photo, and the Mississippi River, seen at the bottom, both contributed to the water that filled the city.

Spencer, the chief engineer for the Orleans Levee District, quoted in a September 21, 2005, *New York Times* article. Given New Orleans's susceptibility to hurricanes, why were the levees not built to sustain maximum-level winds and storm surges? The Army Corps of Engineers was ultimately responsible, though it did face its own obstacles.

After Betsy, the Army Corps proposed a number of projects that were thwarted by activists and city leaders who worried about potentially negative consequences. For example, the Army Corps's first proposal was to build floodgates at the eastern edge of Lake Pontchartrain. These were intended to prevent storm surges from entering the lake in the first place. But a prominent environmental group worried that the floodgates would restrict water circulation and, ultimately, kill the lake. So, it used a legal challenge to prohibit their construction.

A second plan, to build separate floodgates separating the lake from the canal, was met with similar resistance from the city, which was afraid that these gates would prevent the city's sewage department from being able to pump rainwater out of New Orleans. To this day, some former army engineers believe that if either of these floodgates would have been built, they would have prevented much of the Katrina flooding. The story of what went wrong in New Orleans flood prevention is, in part, a story of persistent squabbling between the Army Corps, environmental groups, and political leaders.

It is also a story of chronic environmental neglect. Historically, the Louisiana coast has been home to some of the world's greatest wetlands, areas of saturated soil that are lush with vegetation and make for one of the most effective natural shields against hurricanes. Bogs, marshes, and other types of wetlands act as a kind of "speed bump," slowing storms down as they make their way toward more populated areas. However, between the years 1930 and 2005, nearly one million acres of southern Louisiana wetlands disappeared into the Gulf. Since hurricanes were known to be a constant threat, this coastal erosion helped create a nightmare waiting to happen.

There are several reasons for the wetlands' dramatic decline. First, as historian Douglas Brinkley points out, the Army Corps's decision to channel the Mississippi River toward the Gulf of Mexico had the negative effect of concentrating sediment in the Gulf rather than allowing it to spread across the rest of the coast. Second, oil companies drilled and laid down miles of pipelines across the wetlands, destroying precious environmental infrastructure.

IGNORING THE INEVITABLE

By 2001, public safety officials were well aware of the threat posed by a hurricane. In 2001, just months before the attacks of September 11, a Federal Emergency Management Agency (FEMA) study listed it as one of three disaster scenarios that would wreak the most havoc on the United States. The others included a San Francisco earthquake and, eerily, a terrorist attack on New York City. Later that December, the *Houston Chronicle* predicted what might happen if a Category 3 hurricane ever struck. "The city's less-than-adequate evacuation routes would strand 250,000 people or more, and probably kill one of 10 left behind as the city drowned under 20 feet of water," wrote science writer Eric Berger. "Thousands of refugees could land in Houston. Economically, the toll would be shattering."

Having known that the wetlands were disappearing, that the levee system was inadequate, and that the threat of hurricanes was just as real as it was when Betsy struck in 1965, the federal government behaved for years like a motorist driving on an almost empty tank of gas. Rather than address the root of the problem by funding levee improvements, Congress and the White House left the fate of New Orleans to wishful thinking. Hopefully, the worst-case scenario—in this case, an entire city swept almost completely under the sea—would never come to pass.

But how wishful could anyone's thinking have really been? In July 2004, scientists from Louisiana State University's

Hurricane Center demonstrated what would happen if a Category 3 storm did strike New Orleans. Using computer simulation technology, they unleashed the fictional "Hurricane Pam" on an exact replica of the city. The computer analysis showed the storm topping levees and flooding certain neighborhoods with up to 20 feet of water. By the time the sky cleared in this role-playing exercise, 80 percent of the city's buildings had suffered from serious damage. One million residents had evacuated. Most housing was obliterated. The Hurricane Pam exercise was intended to bring FEMA, the U.S. Army Corps of Engineers, the National Weather Service, and other state and federal agencies together so that they could coordinate a more effective response to a real hurricane; to get them "singing from the same sheet of music," as Terry Tullier, New Orleans's director of emergency preparedness put it in the July 20, 2004, edition of the *New Orleans Times-Picayune.*

When it came to the threat of flooding in New Orleans, Tullier was nothing less than alarmist. "When I do presentations," he told the *New York Times* in August 2002, "I start by saying that when the Big One comes, many of you will die—let's get that out of the way." Speaking to the *New Orleans Times-Picayune* the day after the Hurricane Pam exercise began, Tullier said, "I'm always asked what's my worst nightmare, and I talk about the generations of New Orleanians who have no historical reference in their brain about how bad this will be." Delivered with a gentle Louisiana bayou accent, his next words turned out to be prophetic. "And when I preach the gospel of evacuation, they won't take it seriously."

The word coming from FEMA was more optimistic. "We made great progress this week in our preparedness efforts," FEMA Regional Director Ron Castleman announced shortly after the conclusion of the Pam exercise. "Disaster response teams developed action plans in critical areas such as search and rescue, medical care, sheltering, temporary housing, school restoration and debris management." Hundreds of thousands of New Orleans residents counted on FEMA and state and local agencies to work together to ensure their safety. Being able to work together as a team in a real-life situation,

Levees and floodgates built to keep the floodwaters from New Orleans broke during Hurricane Betsy in 1965. New levees, like the one in this photo, were built to prevent another disaster like Betsy, but were too old to withstand the force of Katrina.

however, was different than working through a computer simulation. Certain challenges would remain unforeseen—for example, knowing which rescue personnel would remain calm, fearless, and dedicated to the course of action and which would ultimately crack under pressure. And in a real-life situation, there were consequences to learning from mistakes—decisions needed to be immediate and decisive, and any slipup could mean the difference between life and death.

While there was no shortage of warnings about the inadequate levee system in the years leading up to Katrina—in addition to the *Houston Chronicle*, articles appeared in *Scientific American*, *National Geographic*, and the *New Orleans Times-Picayune* in the first few years of the 2000s—alarm bells were also being sounded as early as three months before the hurricane struck, according to later reports in the September 4, 2005, *Los Angeles Times*. In May, the New Orleans district of the Army Corps of Engineers told the White House and Congress that a flood-control study that had been proposed four years earlier was never actually carried out due to a lack of funding. Levees had settled and would soon need to be raised, the Army Corps warned. Finally, if a major hurricane did strike New Orleans, storm surges could knock out two of the city's pumping stations, leaving the city unequipped to deal with a flood. Even in ordinary circumstances, the pumping stations were needed to keep the city dry. It does not take an engineer to figure out what would happen if pumping stations failed during a flood. Perhaps the most prominent warning came from Louisiana State University hurricane researcher Ivor van Heerden, who said in July 2005 that "if a hurricane comes next month, New Orleans could no longer exist."

Finally, despite repeated warnings, the leaders of the city of New Orleans, the state of Louisiana, and the United States of America finally faced the situation they all feared on Saturday, August 27. The news was delivered as many tragic messages are—in the early morning. At 5 A.M., the National

Hurricane Center made a sobering announcement. Katrina was a "major hurricane," only expected to grow stronger. Over the next 24 hours, it would veer northwest across the Gulf of Mexico, making a beeline toward the Louisiana and Mississippi coasts.

It was too late to fix New Orleans's frail and inadequate system of levees, too late to fund necessary improvements. Debates about the effectiveness of floodwalls and other measures that might have a hand in flood prevention were no longer productive. Hurricane Katrina was coming, and it was expected to be deadly. The only responsible thing a political leader could do was make sure government resources such as buses and communications lines were secured and that residents were quickly and safely evacuated. The day of reckoning was finally here, and New Orleans had only 48 hours to prepare for it.

3 48 Hours

Louisiana governor Kathleen Blanco was a subdued, serious woman. She won her office a year-and-a-half earlier by framing her political agenda around issues such as improving health care, repairing highways, and bringing jobs to the state. Now she was expected to help organize the response to a large-scale natural disaster, hardly a focal point of the platform she had laid out.

Yet, in the few days that remained before Katrina was set to demolish the Louisiana coast, Blanco did what she could to prod residents to leave and to ensure that lifesaving resources were available when the storm finally touched down. On Friday, she issued a "state of emergency" alert for Louisiana and appeared on CNN, warning viewers that Louisiana was "in the strike zone."

The hurricane had picked up in intensity since Thursday, when it passed through an area just north of Miami, Florida. There, Katrina uprooted trees, knocked down street overpasses, and left at least six people dead. (Eight more deaths were reported later.) It also left a million others stranded without electricity. The scariest thing was that its winds never exceeded 90 mph. By the time Katrina reached the Louisiana Gulf Coast, those winds could reach as much as 155 mph or more. In the meantime, the storm would retreat southeast to the Gulf of Mexico, its temper growing more furious over the warm waters.

The next day, Saturday, Blanco wrote a letter to the White House requesting federal assistance. Emergency shelters needed to be opened, coastal areas needed to be evacuated, and search-and-rescue missions needed to be organized, she wrote to President George Bush. The incident was of "such severity and magnitude," she explained, "that effective response is beyond the capabilities of the State and affected local governments."

President Bush, who had spent the morning delivering a weekly radio address on Middle Eastern politics, granted Blanco's request. He authorized the Department of Homeland Security to coordinate hurricane relief efforts. Homeland Security was the organization created shortly after 9/11 to deal with terrorist attacks and natural disasters. It includes FEMA, the Federal Emergency Management Agency, which under Director Michael Brown had responded to a series of high-profile Florida hurricanes in 2004.

As Blanco lobbied behind the scenes for federal assistance, she remained confident when she spoke to her constituents publicly. Though during a Friday press conference in Jefferson Parish she advised residents to evacuate, she still asserted that "I believe we are prepared. That's the one thing I've always been able to brag about." In fact, Blanco had seen to it that 200 vessels from the Louisiana Department of Wildlife and Fisheries were made available at strategic locations outside of the coastal parishes. Rescuers would be able to use the boats to start helping flood victims immediately. Blanco also authorized the mobilization of 2,000 soldiers and airmen with the Louisiana National Guard, while her department of Social Services identified shelters and Red Cross centers in strategic locations across the state.

Though she was later criticized for leaving Louisiana unprepared, according to author Douglas Brinkley, such precautions seem to indicate that she was better equipped than

New Orleans Mayor Ray Nagin (*left*) and Louisiana governor Kathleen Blanco (*right*) were criticized for being unprepared for Hurricane Katrina. Residents of New Orleans and low-lying areas of Louisiana were told too late to evacuate their homes, contributing to the disaster. Councilman Oliver Thomas stands center.

her counterparts in the city and federal governments—that is, New Orleans mayor Ray Nagin and President George W. Bush—to deal with the coming disaster. Perhaps, when Blanco spoke with such confidence to the people of Jefferson County, she was recognizing the widely held opinion that strong leaders never show weakness. Or, perhaps, her certainty was based on her optimism that the White House and FEMA, having been alerted to the seriousness of Katrina's threat, would respond with all of the determination, the resources, and the power available in the federal government.

By Saturday, Blanco's concern was growing by the hour. That afternoon, she asked an assistant to contact priests, ministers, and other community religious leaders and tell them to instruct their faithful to "Go pray. Go pack." Some listened, some did not. Around 7:25 P.M., she spoke with Max Mayfield, director of the National Hurricane Center in Miami. Mayfield was the top hurricane expert in the country—the "go-to guy" for any public official with storm-related questions. He had been in the business of predicting the weather for more than 30 years, and the signals that were showing up on his radar troubled him deeply.

Katrina was moving northwest at about seven mph, from a spot about 180 miles west of Key West, Florida, Mayfield said. Landfall would occur in southern Louisiana some time in the next 36 hours. He expected Katrina to be at least as devastating as Hurricane Camille, the 1969 storm that killed 143 people in the Gulf Coast and another 113 in Virginia. "I'm sorry," he told the governor, muttering it again and again. "I'm sorry." Speaking later to the *U.S. News and World Report*, a Blanco spokesperson said it was "like he was offering his sympathy before the storm hit because he knew what was coming."

A HESITATION TO EVACUATE

New Orleans mayor Ray Nagin's Saturday began, ominously enough, at a funeral parlor, where he and other Louisiana power brokers were attending services for Clarence Barney, the former director of the New Orleans Urban League.

Though Barney was the center of attention, his memory was not the only thing on people's minds. Two-thirds of the way through the ceremony, former mayor Marc Morial's communications director slipped him a note, according to the filmmaker Spike Lee. "We must leave," it said. "The storm is a Category 5 now." Morial, who lived in New York, would be leaving on an airplane headed far from the Louisiana coast. But Nagin did not have the luxury of simply getting up and flying away. As the city's top-ranking public official, he would have to wait out the storm along with all of the Louisiana residents who had been left behind.

Though most other city administrators planned to take refuge from the storm in the emergency command center they had fashioned on the ninth floor of City Hall, Nagin chose to stay on the top floor of the 27-story Hyatt hotel. Far above the city's streets, this was hardly the vantage point from which many in the Lower Ninth Ward would face the storm—on the upper floors of poorly designed, ramshackle houses, where the sounds of the crashing glass and the howling winds and the sight of bodies swept away by the surge would be immediate. By setting up his headquarters so far aboveground, he established the perfect metaphor for a government response seemingly removed from the needs of ordinary New Orleanians.

The mayor cut out from the funeral early for a City Hall press conference. Nagin was tall, goateed, and had a shaved head. His style was exceptionally casual. He spoke colloquially, peppering his speech with expressions such as "doggone" or "man." He came across as a "regular" guy in the laid-back town where he governed, but Katrina was anything but a relaxed situation. Mustering up a more somber tone, the mayor warned that "although the track could change, forecasters believe Hurricane Katrina will affect New Orleans. . . . Citizens need to begin preparing now so they will be ready to leave when necessary. Do everything to prepare for a regular hurricane, but treat this one differently because it is headed our way," he continued. "This is not a test."

Nagin advised residents in low-lying areas such as Algiers and the Lower Ninth Ward to begin evacuating immediately. For everyone else, he recommended the following: board windows, remove backyard trash, and stock up on food and bottled water. These were all reasonable suggestions, but they fell short of a mandatory evacuation, the ultimate safeguard that a mayor can demand. If Nagin was not taking the most dramatic precaution available, how bad could the storm *really* be? Only a mandatory evacuation would scare otherwise stubborn residents into leaving, and even then, there would still be holdouts. Many residents were old enough to have survived Hurricane Betsy and felt that if they could survive that storm, they could handle this one, too. As one New Orleanian explained in an article for the North Carolina–based *Independent Weekly*, "When you live on the Gulf Coast, you get used to hurricane warnings . . . there are two to four serious storms every year."

True, Tropical Storm Cindy had swept through the Louisiana Gulf region that July. There was no major damage, save about a dozen flooded homes. Seven years earlier, the eye of Hurricane Georges fell about 90 miles northeast of New Orleans, near Biloxi, Mississippi. Again, the storm's 105-mph winds caused moderate damage to some of the city's buildings, but it was hardly severe. Katrina, on the other hand, was expected to be a monster, quite literally a killer. So why did Nagin not issue a mandatory evacuation, like nearby St. Charles and Plaquemines parishes had done on Saturday?

According to *Times-Picayune* reporter Bruce Nolan, the mayor was worried about being sued by hotels and other businesses that relied heavily upon tourist dollars for their income. If the evacuation caused these businesses to lose money, they might demand compensation from the city. Nagin did not want to put the local government in a position of owing these businesses money. It is probably safe to say that this was not the right thing to be thinking about during such a time of crisis. Waiting to hear back from his legal team, Nagin squandered precious time that could have been spent getting residents out of the city and, possibly, saving lives. He said that he might call for a "voluntary" evacuation later in the afternoon or early the next morning when traffic lanes were redirected to accommodate outgoing traffic exclusively. "This will give people more options to leave the area," he said. "However, citizens need to begin preparing now so they will be ready to leave when necessary."

There was a certain irony to the suggestion that citizens prepare now, less than two days before the hurricane. While everybody needed to have a personal evacuation plan, the overarching strategy that guided the city's response was even more important. Unfortunately, the job of fully organizing that strategy had been largely overlooked.

The city actually had a "Comprehensive Emergency Management Plan" that had been put together in 2000, two years before Nagin took office. Only 14 pages long, the plan did address the issue of evacuations. Residents who could not otherwise leave on their own due to age, income, or disability restrictions were to be taken care of by the city. City officials should utilize all "available resources" to assist evacuation efforts, the emergency plan stated, making "special arrangements . . . to evacuate persons unable to transport themselves or who require specific lifesaving assistance." A separate state emergency response plan, revised in 2000 and signed off on by then-governor Marc Morial, suggested that school and municipal buses be used for evacuation purposes.

New Orleans had at least 364 municipal buses and hundreds of other school buses at its disposal, according to the September 8, 2005, *Houston Chronicle*. The municipal buses alone could have transported about 22,000 people per run, according to estimates cited in the *New Orleans Times-Picayune*.

While this still seemed a grossly inadequate means of evacuating the 134,000 people known to lack access to transportation, it would have been something. But under Nagin's watch, the city made the critical mistake of leaving these buses on low ground where they would be trapped in the coming flood. To make matters worse, Amtrak even offered to allow the city to take advantage of its last run out of New Orleans, but the city declined. At 8:30 P.M., a "ghost train" left the station, not a seat filled among the hundreds that were available. By Saturday night, the city's poor had no practical choice but to stick around town and hope for the best. As for the elderly—well,

Nagin had asked residents to take the responsibility to check up on older friends and family members and make sure they had evacuation plans.

The next time the mayor spoke to reporters, at 5:00 P.M., he was joined by Governor Blanco. Joint appearances were somewhat awkward for the mayor and governor. That is because Nagin, a Democrat, had chosen to support Blanco's Republican opponent during her gubernatorial campaign. It was an unusual move that left Blanco feeling bitter toward the mayor. Nevertheless, the hurricane required the two of them to act as a team, and together Nagin and Blanco put up a united front, urging New Orleanians once again to evacuate

Residents who did not evacuate New Orleans before Hurricane Katrina hit were forced to find shelter at the Superdome, the city's sports and entertainment facility. Many managed to find their way there by wading through the floodwaters or using whatever was around to help them.

the city—*voluntarily*. "This is not a test. This is the real deal," Nagin warned. "We want you to take this a little more seriously and start moving—right now, as a matter of fact." For those who had no way of getting out, they said that the Superdome, the city's 70,000-capacity indoor sports and entertainment facility, would be opened as a "shelter of last resort." In all of New Orleans, it was the only facility that could sustain hurricane winds of Category 3 or higher.

The Superdome was normally festive—a place to take in a New Orleans Saints football game or a rock concert. But now, city officials had transformed it into something somber: a place of sheer survival. People who intended to take up refuge there were advised to plan as if it were a camping trip—to bring three or four days' worth of food, drinks, folding chairs, and other items that might make the stay more comfortable. Other rules applied as well: "No weapons, no large items."

In the days immediately following the hurricane, issues of law and order would take center stage. A hurricane was, after all, a dream come true for petty criminals. It allowed thieves to operate in emptied-out cities where windows were shattered and electronic surveillance and security systems were shut down. While police saved lives, looters could have their run of abandoned homes and businesses.

In some ways, though, petty criminals were the least of law-abiding New Orleanians' worries. Rapists, kidnappers, and murderers could also operate freely in a chaotic and lawless environment. The stress caused by hurricane survival could add to the problems by making otherwise rational people act out in violent or irresponsible ways.

With this in mind, Nagin's chief of police, Eddie Compass, had a few announcements he wanted to make. A 26-year-veteran of the department, Compass anticipated that the same types of problems that occurred shortly after Betsy would again reappear after Katrina. His leadership would be just as important as Nagin's in coming days, and one of his first major announcements was that the city would be imposing a curfew on citizens in the wake of the storm. It would also position police officers at local shopping centers, dealing with looters "severely and harshly" and prosecuting them "to the fullest extent of the law."

Worn out from all of the worry and commotion, Nagin retired to his home. That evening, his cell phone rang. It was Max Mayfield from the National Hurricane Center, and he sounded alarmed. Mandatory evacuation was called for at once, the weather director told the mayor. Apparently, it was just the wake-up call that the mayor needed. "He scared the 'you know what' out of me," Nagin later recalled, speaking to WDSU-Channel 6. It was not the first such warning Mayfield had delivered that day. Earlier, he had spoken with Blanco and Mississippi governor Haley Barbour. "The thing I remember telling all three of them is that when I walked out of the hurricane center that night I wanted to be able to sleep at night knowing that I had done everything that I could do," Mayfield later remembered.

By the next morning, the storm was Category 5, and Nagin and Blanco were on television, urging a *mandatory* evacuation of Orleans parish. There were less than 24 hours until landfall. "We're facing the storm most of us have feared," Nagin said. "This is going to be an unprecedented event," he warned, adding that storm surges would likely "topple" the levees.

In moments such as these, Nagin showed that he understood the scope of the catastrophe ahead. But speaking later that same day to CNN, he seemed oblivious to the tragedy's human consequences. Thousands of lives were in jeopardy, yet Nagin told the network that "the real issue that I don't think the nation is paying attention to" is that of oil. New Orleans was responsible for nearly a third of all the oil produced in the United States. "So, this can have a significant impact on oil prices going forward." Perhaps nobody in government realized exactly what was in store for the city of New Orleans and the entire Gulf Coast region.

President George Bush was vacationing at his Crawford, Texas, ranch as he kept track of the storm developments. At noon, he participated in a videoconference with regional officials and federal leaders including FEMA Director Michael Brown and Homeland Security Chief Michael Chertoff. Hurricane expert Mayfield took center stage of the discussions, putting up slides that illustrated exactly where the storm and its deadly surges might impact the Gulf region. He was especially worried about New Orleans. "I don't think anyone can tell you right now with any confidence whether the levees will be topped or not," Mayfield said. "That's obviously a very, very grave concern."

Brown was worried that FEMA was not prepared for the disaster ahead. He warned of a "catastrophe within a catastrophe" unfolding at the Superdome, with medics unequipped to respond to health issues and a roof that might not hold. His anxieties seemed to be lost on the president, who did not have a single question for any officials attending the meeting. Calmly and assuredly, he told state leaders that the federal government was prepared to provide them with "whatever resources and assets" it had at its disposal both before and after the storm.

That afternoon, he appeared on television, warning people that, "We cannot stress enough the danger this hurricane poses to Gulf Coast communities." He continued: "I urge all citizens to put their own safety and the safety of their families first by moving to safe ground. Please listen carefully to instructions provided by state and local officials."

THE CITY TAKES SHELTER

That afternoon, tens of thousands of cars lined up on the highways and caused standstill traffic for most of the drive away from the Louisiana coast. Besides New Orleans, other communities along the northern Gulf Coast states of Louisiana, Mississippi, and Alabama issued evacuation orders, bringing the total number of affected residents to approximately 1.2 million people, according to FEMA data.

As the region's highways became congested with automobiles, a separate exodus took place within city limits as the poor, elderly, and disabled made their way to the Louisiana Superdome. While some arrived on buses provided by FEMA to the Louisiana National Guard, others simply walked. One resident, Michael Skipper, dragged along a wagon brimming only with clothes and a small radio. "The good stuff—the television and the furniture—you just have to hope something's there when you get back. If it's not, you just start over," he told an AP reporter. Another man, 42-year-old Joey Branson, brought only a fresh-baked apple pie and a paperback mystery novel. "That's all I need," he said, smiling. Collectively, they

The Superdome became a shelter for the residents of New Orleans who couldn't leave the city. Louisiana National Guardsmen were brought in to help control the crowd—some believed too aggressively.

waited patiently to get inside the arena, a scene the Associated Press painted with an eye for physical detail:

> The sickest among them didn't flee the 160-mph wrath of Hurricane Katrina on Sunday as much as they hobbled to safety on crutches, canes and on stretchers. Others lined up for blocks, clutching meager belongings and crying children as National Guardsman searched them for guns, knives and drugs.

The last part of this description really bothered NBC reporter Brian Williams. As they frisked people coming into the stadium, some of the National Guardsmen were "being quite rough" physically as well as verbally. "It felt bad," Williams recalled in a broadcast a year later, on August 28, 2006. "The men were being aggressively patted down. I asked why? I was told, 'Well, they're looking for cigarette lighters to enforce the ban on smoking inside the Superdome.'" At a time when compassion and empathy would have gone a long way, some security officers acted militaristic—not exactly unexpected from the Department of Homeland Security, an organization accustomed to dealing with threats from terrorists.

Still, despite the masses of people who had either fled in cars or hobbled their way to the Superdome, thousands remained holed up in their homes in New Orleans and nearby parishes. Recalling his ordeal later for the Minneapolis/St. Paul *City Pages*, 24-year-old Cory Delany explained how he actually moved with his parents and sister from the outskirts of the city into his aunt's house at the heart of the "bowl." Unlike his parents' home, his aunt's building had two stories. Just east of the Lower Ninth Ward, in St. Bernard Parish, dozens of elderly residents remained bedridden or wheelchair-bound at St. Rita's nursing home. The owners doubted the storm was going to be as bad as expected, and they evidently did not want to spend the time and effort required to move the mostly immobile residents to a different location.

By Sunday evening, holdouts could also be found in the Mississippi towns of Bay St. Louis, Waveland, Gulfport, and Biloxi. If nothing else, they could be consoled by the words of FEMA Director Michael Brown, who had earlier spoken to CNN with the same kind of confidence exhibited by President Bush and Governor Blanco. "We are ready. We are going to respond," he promised millions of Americans. "We're going to do whatever it takes to help victims. . . . We're going to lean forward as far as possible and do everything we can to help those folks in Louisiana, Alabama and Mississippi."

4 An Unrelenting Force

When describing the sound of a hurricane, a writer has no shortage of metaphors from which to choose. The television cameraman Jim Zura, who was holed up in Texas during 1983's Hurricane Alicia, wrote on his Web site of the "deep, insidious, intense, powerful roar" of the Category 3 storm, which "sounds absolutely demonic, like a mean, ill-willed chant." Historian Douglas Brinkley compared the sound to "the grating pitch a dentist's suction cup makes after it's extracted the last molecule of spittle from your mouth . . . a dry vacuum drone that over a two- or three-hour period starts chiseling away at your morale." Reporting from the Superdome, NBC's Brian Williams compared the sounds that began shortly after 6:00 A.M. to "a New York city subway train." Others said they thought it was "thunder or someone hammering." Whatever was heard by the thousands of people stranded in the Superdome early Monday morning, it was not just chiseling away at their morale—it was hacking away at the roof. By 10:30 A.M., Katrina had peeled off a large portion of the roof's rubberized covering, exposing the steel skull underneath.

Nobody worried about the Superdome blowing away completely. But the threat of the roof caving in was something that the building's managers had fretted about privately in the days leading up to the storm. They wondered how appropriate it would be to house evacuees there after all. First problem: temperature. Even though the building had emergency generators, in the almost inevitable case of a power outage, they were not hooked up to air conditioners. The people taking shelter there would have to endure temperatures of 90°F (32°C) or more. To make matters worse, these generators could only handle low-power emergency lighting. As soon as power went out, the vast arena would be illuminated only by a dim and ghastly glow. Finally, in the equally likely case that water pressure failed, nobody would be able to use the bathrooms. A shortage of water combined with sweltering heat was a dangerous, deadly combination. "We can make things very nice for 75,000 people for four hours," Superdome regional vice president Doug Thornton told the Associated Press on Sunday. "But we aren't really set up to really accommodate 8,000 for four days."

Nevertheless, evacuees managed to remain optimistic Sunday evening. When an official addressed the crowd to let them know food had arrived, everybody cheered. That optimism was tested, however, when the power went out and the fresh water stopped running. Building managers' worst fears about the roof were also coming to be realized. Katrina had torn two holes right through it, and water began pouring into a section of the arena. In a way, it was strangely welcome—the holes were the building's only source of daylight.

With no way of checking up on the outside world—cell phone reception was virtually nonexistent—thousands were left wondering if their homes were still standing or if their friends and relatives had survived the storm. The Superdome had become a holding facility, and National Guard troops were not allowing people to leave. Since many parts of the city were not yet flooded, this did not make a lot of sense to reporters such as Brian Williams. And so much for that lighter ban that National Guardsmen had enforced so dutifully as evacuees

Residents were eager to return to their homes to assess the damage of the storm, but thousands of people were forced to remain at the Superdome by the Louisiana National Guard. Other shelters in New Orleans, including the convention center, were also full of people waiting for buses to transport them to shelters in nearby states that offered assistance.

made their way into the building—evacuees were each given a pack of matches with the military-style meals passed out twice each day by Guardsmen. It was the first of a series of contradictions—things that just did not make sense.

The fact that officials were so tight-lipped with information bothered the veteran newscaster. "I get that there was no power," Williams went on to say later. "But where were the bullhorns? Where were the National Guardsmen to say, 'Folks, the bulk of the storm is over? We understand the damage so far is not severe in the city of New Orleans.' But they somehow didn't deserve that." Williams had nightmares about his experiences in New Orleans, and this was probably true of others now stuck in this "refuge of last resort." Unfortunately, their terror was only beginning.

The nightmare was also just starting for those who took cover in less sturdy homes across the city—people such as Cory Delany and his family. Very quickly, they realized Cory's aunt's home was not safe. "The whole house expanded like it was going to blow up, then it just went black," the 24-year-old told the Minneapolis/St. Paul *City Pages*. "Then the water went to coming up, got into the house. It got so high to where everything on the bottom floor was floating. It got up to about the fifth step going upstairs." Delany and his family, including his mother who suffers from multiple sclerosis, had no choice but to flee to the second floor. Now the only thing the Delanys could hope for was that the floodwaters would recede rather than rise.

Further up the Gulf Coast, in Biloxi, Mississippi, the situation was equally dire. The rain pounded like a drum roll on Hardy Jackson's rooftop, and the 53-year-old grandfather knew there was nothing he could do now except drink coffee, pace back and forth, and hope that his house's wooden frame would not give way to the 145-mph winds and floodwaters coming in from the south. The city's mayor had already shut down each of Biloxi's 10 casinos, the economic lifeblood of the small community, and most of its 51,000 residents had fled for safer ground. Yet Jackson had chosen not to leave the area as the

Abandoned Pumps

Pumping water out of New Orleans became a futile task after Katrina demolished the city's levee system. Any water that mechanics tried to pump into Lake Pontchartrain just came right back into the city. So, New Orleans abandoned its pumping stations after the 17th Street Canal breach. But just east of New Orleans, in Jefferson Parish, pumping out water could have saved houses and perhaps even lives lost to flooding—yet this pumping was called off during the critical daylight hours on Monday by Parish president Aaron Broussard. Pump mechanics were sent to a parish 110 miles away and did not get back until the early evening.

Residents were furious when they found out the stations had been closed. "I believe our homes would not have flooded in Hurricane Katrina had the pumps been running at the proper time. Now we have the agony—yes, agony—of trying to meet with insurance adjusters, fighting mold and mildew, and throwing our treasured possessions in a heap on the curb," one angry homeowner told the *Times-Picayune*. "What kind of faith can we have in our public officials to protect us?" In the wake of criticism, Broussard stood by his decision. He said that leaving pump operators at their posts amounted to a "death sentence" for those workers. In the future, the newspaper has suggested, the parish ought to work to find shelters for the workers that are closer to the parish and to offer more money to workers who accept the risk of staying on duty during hurricanes. Nevertheless, he faced a tough decision—one that ultimately required a decision to endanger the lives of some citizens for the sake of others. In disaster or in war, these are the toughest decisions political leaders face.

government had advised. It was ironic. Instead of staying in a home that would protect him from the storm, Hardy Jackson stayed behind so that he could protect his home. Though his children had already evacuated, his wife, Tonette, remained by his side.

The couple's residence was especially flood-prone. Just a block away from the water, it stood close enough for them to smell its salty breeze. But aroma is not what alerted them to Katrina's imminent presence. Instead, it was sound—the thunderous crash of a storm surge bursting through the walls. Within seconds, Jackson found himself floating alongside fallen branches and street litter. Thinking quickly, he and Tonette escaped to their daughter's second-floor bedroom. But they recognized that the second story would not remain dry for long, so they continued moving to higher ground—this time, to the attic. Hardy looked out of an air vent and saw his house filling up like a bathtub. Everything he owned would be waterlogged, lost, or destroyed completely. The only thing he had to save now was his wife's life, as well as his own.

He punched a hole in the roof, the only safe place left to go. Then, he and Tonette climbed out. From their bird's-eye view, the Jacksons would have seen the surge swallowing the homes in their neighborhood. With wind lashing against her cheeks and bludgeoning her eardrums, Tonette held onto her husband's hand for dear life. Then, the house split into two between them.

After the storm finally passed, a local TV news reporter found Jackson wandering hopelessly with his young son by his side. "I tried. I, I hold her hand tight as I could, and she told me you can't hold me," he told the reporter for CBS affiliate WKRG. "She said take care of the kids and the grandkids and my kids." With those final words etched forever in his memory, Hardy watched helplessly as his wife's body was swept away. He clung to a tree for safety, where he remained for hours until a neighbor helped him down.

Back in New Orleans, the years of poor flood planning had finally come home to roost. Between the hours of 5:00 and 8:00 A.M., levees were breached in several places along the Industrial Canal and the Mississippi River Gulf Outlet (MRGO). Gulf waters were pushed westward from Lake Borgne, as well as along the MRGO and straight into the Industrial Canal. Neighborhoods in New Orleans East, St. Bernard Parish, and the Lower Ninth Ward were flooded. Within a few more hours, levees breached at the 17th Street and London Avenue canals, causing water to begin pouring out into neighborhoods there.

Flooding along the Gulf Coast continued even after Katrina had left the area. Covering 80 percent of New Orleans, the floods damaged and destroyed homes, buildings, and roads. Though the cost of damage varies, estimates of federal officials and insurance companies range in the billions.

Calls began pouring into the city's "911" hotline. Entire families were stuck in attics, with no way to break open the ceiling to climb out onto the roof. Operators tried their best to keep their composure, but with limited rescue resources available, there was little they could do but offer simple advice—"get to higher ground" or "try standing on furniture." Reporting for the *Dallas Morning News*, journalists Karen Brooks and Pete Slover described "despairing operators . . . forced to listen to what they later described as 'death calls,' the terrifying sounds of mothers crying for help while holding their babies out of rooftops for air, succumbing to the waters and dropping to their deaths while horrified operators listened. Callers were stranded in burning apartments with no way for trucks to get to them."

Police officer Chris Abbott was in his Lakeview home when the 17th Street levee broke, and he called fellow officers at the New Orleans Police Department headquarters for some advice on how to get out of the predicament in which he now found himself—in his attic and up to his neck in water. Abbott was a tough cop who had survived being shot in the line of duty four years earlier. But now he found himself helpless. "I'm getting tired," he said over his police radio. "I don't know if I'm going to make it out in time."

Captain Jimmy Scott began to give him instructions: First, find the attic vent and try to push or punch it out. Abbot said he could not do it. "I don't think I'm going to make it," he said again. He began thanking his police colleagues for everything they had done for him. As Abbott behaved nobly in the face of death, Captain Scott refused to give up on his fellow officer. He asked if Abbott had his weapon. He did. Thinking quickly, the captain instructed Abbot to shoot all 45 rounds of his pistol into the base of the attic vent. That would weaken the foundation enough for him to be able to push his way out. No sooner than Captain Scott had said those potentially lifesaving words, the phone went silent. For several

Her Name's Not Katrina

Before weather forecasters anticipated the coming of the summer's biggest storm, Stephenie Post thought she would be resting quietly at Mississippi's Keesler Medical Center on August 29, preparing for a scheduled cesarean section operation the next day. While the 39-week-pregnant mother of one did find herself at the hospital along with her husband Aaron, an Air Force pilot, and two-year-old daughter Austin, her stay was anything but ordinary, according to a report on the U.S. Air Force Web site. First, the power went out when a storm surge wiped out the hospital's basement generators. As Post tried to carry her daughter upstairs in the darkness, she tripped and fell. Her water broke and she went into labor.

Doctors had to think quickly. There was no way to airlift her out of the hospital because the winds were too strong. So, the medical staff quickly improvised a delivery room in the

agonizing minutes, the officers at police headquarters spoke into the transmitter, asking "Chris, are you OK?" After five minutes had gone by, Abbott reemerged alive and triumphant. His words were a much-needed boost of confidence during an otherwise disheartening situation. "I'm halfway out," Abbott said triumphantly. "I'm going to make it."

Back at the Hyatt where Mayor Nagin was staying, hundreds of windows had blown out on the building's north side. From a distance it looked like a giant honeycomb, with tiny handkerchiefs hanging from each of the cells. These were actually curtains. They had become mangled and wind-torn by the wrath of the storm. Nagin and fellow city officials had trouble communicating during the storm. A shard of glass had intensive care unit, moving around furniture and dragging in equipment. They wiped everything down with antiseptic solution to make sure everything was sanitary, and then surgeons began the operation, guided by industrial-strength flashlights. "I wasn't really scared about the delivery. I was confident that these people knew what they were doing," Post told Air Force reporters, "but I was in a lot of pain, and I was ready for it to be over with."

Post delivered a healthy, eight-pound, nine-ounce girl who they named Sage Madison. Post said she wanted "something original that wasn't hard to pronounce." Though "Katrina" might also fit that criteria, the couple realized the experience of giving birth to their second daughter is a great contrast to what others faced during the storm. "We wanted everyone to know that with all of the horrible things that Katrina did to Keesler [Medical Center], something really good came out of it—our daughter."

punctured a backup generator powering the city's emergency communications radio system. It eventually shut down completely. Nagin and his staff tried to use satellite phones, but their batteries ran out. Fortunately, quick thinking on the part of Scott Domke, one of the city's technology advisers, restored communications capabilities. Hooking a laptop up to a working electrical socket in the Hyatt conference room, Domke was able to get eight individual lines running from a single Internet-based telephone account.

SPARED FROM CATASTROPHE?

Within hours of the storm's passing, there were reports of breached levees, flooding, and destruction as far as the eye could see. Evacuees remained holed up at the Superdome, and Mayor Nagin reported that at least 200 people were stranded in attics or on rooftops. Despite all of this, some initial newspaper reports about the hurricane were marked with a sense of relief. "Katrina Misses New Orleans, Heavily Damages Mississippi," read the next-day headline in the *New York Times*. A competing daily, *Newsday*, featured the pumped-up title "Spared from Catastrophe." Appearing on the *Today Show* Monday morning, Mayor Nagin prematurely assessed that New Orleans "is still not out of the woods as it relates to the worst-case scenario," but that overall, "it looks as though everyone is pretty safe here and I'm sure that we're going to get through this OK." Even Governor Kathleen Blanco conceded that "it could have been worse," though she cautioned that the lack of communications, power, and passable roads made it too dangerous for evacuees to begin returning.

The *New Orleans Times-Picayune*, the newspaper that covered the storm so thoroughly and diligently that it went on to earn two Pulitzer prizes, offered the more sobering and realistic headline: "Catastrophic: Lakeview Levee Breach Threatens to Inundate City." It would have been on the front page of the paper if a storm had not wiped out the printing press. Instead, the headline only appeared online, to be read by the parts of the country that still had Internet connections.

How many people had died in the hurricane? Nobody knew, but judging from the calls received by emergency workers, there were bound to be some. New Orleans Homeland Security Director Terry Ebbert said as much during an interview with the *New Orleans Times-Picayune*, but in a moment of ill-timed insensitivity, he added that "Everybody who had a way or wanted to get out of the way of this storm was able to. For some that didn't, it was their last night on this earth."

Fatigue and frustration likely contributed to the homeland security director's terse statement, but he would have been

Residents who did not evacuate their homes were forced to destroy the roofs of their houses to avoid the floodwaters. People around the world watched as hurricane victims were plucked from their homes by helicopters or gathered in rescue boats.

hard-pressed repeating it to the families of the elderly residents who had been left helplessly marooned by their caretakers at St. Rita's nursing home. It is almost too much to imagine the profoundly sad scene that took place as waters began rising inside the St. Bernard Parish facility.

The *Dallas Morning News* reported that after floodwaters receded, "the body of one elderly woman, clothed in a thin housedress" could be found on the concrete floor of the front patio. Another thin, bony old man was spread out over the back of a chair when rescuers found his lifeless body. A "blackened hand" stuck out from between a gurney and collapsed wall. One rescuer, 60-year-old Raymond Couture, called it "the worst thing I've ever seen." That was a lot coming from someone who, during Hurricane Betsy, had dragged dead bodies to a levee. Rescuers recovered a total of 34 corpses, plus another body later found in a wooded area behind the home. They were so badly decomposed by the time rescuers got to them that the coroner had no way of figuring out the exact cause of death. Autopsy reports cited it simply as "Katrina-related." Prosecutors sought to hold owners Salvador and Mabel Mangano accountable for their actions, charging them with one count each of negligent homicide for every person who died under their care.

While it was too late to rescue anyone from St. Rita's, the goal of rescuers moving forward was to get as many people out of their homes as possible and drop them off at the Superdome. From there, at least according to what Mayor Nagin had anticipated, FEMA could pick up the job of transferring evacuees from New Orleans to someplace safe. Nagin was expecting a lot from the agency, providing them with what he called "a hell of a list" of requested emergency-related items and services.

FEMA was concerned that dozens or hundreds of different rescue groups working in New Orleans at once could quickly spiral into chaos. So, the agency issued a statement requesting fire departments and other emergency rescue teams to stay away from New Orleans unless they had been explicitly authorized by state or local officials. FEMA was actually turning rescuers away from the city, an early example of what critics considered to be excessive caution and playing "by the books" when improvisation was needed.

By nightfall Monday, the waters were still rising in many parts of the city, and the most difficult part of the rescue effort was yet to come.

5 Heroes, Victims, and Looters

Sergeant Aaron Monceaux was one of the early rescuers to arrive on the scene. The Louisiana Department of Wildlife and Fisheries (LDWF) sergeant's day job was mellow compared to what was expected of him now. Normally, he would cruise through Louisiana's bayou in a small boat, handing out tickets to hunters or fishers operating without a license. On Tuesday, though, Monceaux found himself and several hundred of his LDWF colleagues navigating through floodwater that was littered with corpses; fallen power lines; and scraps of homes, trees, and other floating debris. Monceaux's job was to skim along the surface and find survivors among the wreckage—to seek out the rooftops that jutted out of the water like reeds and rescue those stranded on top or inside of them.

From the second floor of what the Associated Press's Adam Nossiter described as a "trim pastel-green cottage," he sighted terrified onlookers peering out from over a balcony and beckoning for help. Like many others who had been left stranded, they had been waiting all night and morning to capture rescuers' attention. It's hard to imagine how desperate all of New Orleans's remaining residents must have felt after a night of being trapped in their homes. Some had witnessed their own family members drowning. Others spent panicked hours tending to elderly mothers, fathers, and grandparents who had gone more than a day and a half in the stifling sun, with no food, water, or medicine. In impoverished countries, such situations are all too common. But in the United States, the wealthiest, most powerful country in the world, few could imagine that such a thing was even possible.

For many of Katrina's victims, coming to terms with the fact that entire homes and personal possessions had been swept away in the flood was bad enough. But many, including a heavyset woman who Monceaux tried to lower gently from the balcony into his boat, were also troubled by a more immediate anxiety—they did not know how to swim. In a city that was almost entirely submerged, few things could be as terrifying. With Monceaux's small boat rocking unsteadily, the woman began to panic as the officer tried to lower her inside. Thinking quickly, Monceaux told her a joke as he brought her to safety. Realizing she was going to be all right, Loretha Woods took a moment to count blessings. "There is a God. He answers prayers," the AP quoted her. "All that material stuff, we can get back. We've got our life."

Saving lives was the top concern of LDWF rescue workers in the days immediately following the breach of the levees. Though they brought out cadaver dogs trained to sniff for dead bodies, rescue workers generally left corpses where they were, instead focusing their efforts on those who still had a chance to live. They used axes and chainsaws to free people from their cavernous attic hideaways.

Some of the most challenging rescues involved the large numbers of New Orleans area Katrina victims who were trapped in big public buildings. According to the *Baton Rouge Advocate*, 500 evacuees had taken refuge in the Chalmette High School. In St. Bernard Parish, another 600 holed up in the courthouse. At the medical center, there were 350 more. In the first two days of rescue efforts, LDWF officials estimated

Terrified residents are helped from their homes by police officers and good samaritans *(above)*. Much of the New Orleans Police Department was overwhelmed by calls from people in distress, and other municipal services were mobilized to help with rescue efforts.

that their rescue teams had saved at least 3,000 residents in the parishes of Orleans, St. Tammany, and St. Bernard.

With the LDWF on the water, the U.S. Coast Guard took to the air. The agency's daring rescues made for some of the most compelling footage on television. Orange and white helicopters darted across the sky like dragonflies, looking for homes containing stranded residents. Once they found people to rescue, they hovered over the homes and lowered rescuers down in giant steel baskets. They loaded victims, one person at a time, and reeled these baskets back up to the aircraft. It was a slow and skilled process, but the Coast Guard executed it with relentless precision. They worked around-the-clock and stopped only to refuel.

Just as remarkable, people with no emergency training whatsoever came out to assist with the rescue efforts. With nothing more than a 16-foot boat and the help of a determined friend, one New Orleans resident, Eric Charles, managed to save 100 people himself. Charles and his assistant started picking up evacuees at 1:30 P.M. Monday and did not stop until the sun went down. "They gave priority to women and children," the *Advocate* reported, though this two-man rescue squad eventually went back for stranded men. Another rescuer, Michael Knight, continued working even after the sun went down, taking note of the locations of people he could pick up in the morning daylight. Knight told the author Douglas Brinkley that he rescued up to 20 people at a time in his 20-foot, banana-yellow Sea Ray pirogue (pronounced "pee-row"). Blasting reggae music from his boat as he worked, Knight managed to pick up 250 people from the Seventh Ward, including many from a massive housing project, by week's end.

Rescuers such as Knight and Charles came to be known as "The Cajun Navy." One of these homegrown heroes told *The Nation* magazine how he brought a small boat up from the heart of Acadiana, French-speaking southern Louisiana, to help residents stranded in the city. "You know, we were all watching New Orleans on television and we realized that somebody's got to help all these people, because nothing was happening. Nothing," Edna Fontenot recalled. "Then there was a call [by the Louisiana Department of Wildlife and Fisheries] for small boats. So I said 'I'm going.' I knew I could do something. I lived in New Orleans and know how to get around on water. . . . There was no FEMA, just a big ol' bunch of Cajun guys in their boats," he told the magazine. "We tried to coordinate best we could, but it was still chaos. It was steaming hot and there was a smell of death. The people on the rooftops and overpasses were desperate. They had been there for several days in the sun with no food, no water. They were dehydrated, blistered and sick . . . giving up, you know, ready to die." He stayed for two days, until floating debris damaged his propeller. Eric Charles agrees that the experience was challenging emotionally. "It was horrible," he told the *Baton Rouge Advocate*. "People were panicking all over. They didn't know when the water would stop rising."

With all the newly rescued victims, the Superdome's population ballooned to more than 20,000 in a matter of days, and the situation grew to be unbearable. With no usable toilet facilities at their disposal, people had taken to relieving themselves in plain sight of everybody huddled inside the arena. The lack of air-conditioning and ventilation, combined with the stifling Louisiana heat, made for a stench that was close to unbearable—a "sewer," as many people described it. People confined to wheelchairs were lined up in rows of five against the arena's walls. Evacuees dependent upon prescription medications did not have access to pills or other treatments needed to maintain their health.

Still, in spite of the horrible situation, most people remained patient and calm. They played cards, read books, or even napped on the concrete floor in order to pass the slow-moving time. One Superdome resident told the filmmaker Spike Lee how one evacuee lifted spirits with a display of true camaraderie. When suffering was nearing its worst, he led a parade of Gospel music-singing evacuees around the arena. Together, they belted out the words to a traditionally uplifting and empowering African-American spiritual: *This little light of mine, I'm gonna let it shine—let it shine, let it shine, let it shine.* Seeing and hearing this choir was "powerful," the resident said, because it showed how so many weary victims, many of them Christians, put their faith in the hands of God. "After we marched around one time, we go on the outside, and at that time I felt the movement—like the Civil Rights movement."

National Guardsmen eventually began letting people sleep outside on the concourse. Stepping out into the fresh air on Tuesday, 33-year-old Robin Smith told the Associated Press,

Wal-Mart

Corporate retail chain Wal-Mart stood among the heroes that emerged from Hurricane Katrina. Equipped with its own hurricane-tracking software, the company began stocking up on clothing, water, and durable food such as Pop-Tarts as early as August 24. The company planned meticulously, loading trucks for delivery a day before landfall and even securing a special line at a gas station to ensure that deliveries could flow seamlessly, according to the September 6, 2005, *Washington Post*. When the storm hit, the company responded quickly, sending 1,900 truckloads of water and emergency supplies and opening area stores to emergency relief workers. Wal-Mart stores became supply depots, and the company even rushed to set up "mini-Wal Marts" in weather-beaten areas. It also donated an additional $20 million in cash to relief charities. Wal-Mart employees who lost jobs in the Gulf region were promised employment at other Wal-Mart locations. Speaking to the *Post*, one Brookhaven, Mississippi, Chamber of Commerce official commented that, "They were ready before FEMA was."

"It's the first time I've wanted to breathe all day." Unfortunately, the concourse was the furthest she or anyone else could go. Like a moat around a prison, water had begun rising around the Superdome—up to a level of about three feet. On second thought, comparing the Superdome to a prison is even overly generous. As a man who once spent three months in jail on a drunken-driving charge explained to Joseph B. Treaster of the *New York Times*, the Superdome was actually worse than

As one of the few places of refuge in the city, conditions at the New Orleans Superdome quickly deteriorated as toilets and electricity failed and the temperature started to climb. Seen here after the evacuees left, the arena housed more than 15,000 people for five days.

lockup. "In prison you have a place to urinate, a place for other bathroom needs," Michael Childs told the newspaper reporter. "Here you get no water, no toilets, no lights. You get all that in prison."

You also get more security, and you do not have to worry about thousands of strangers sharing the sleeping space around you at night. Rumors quickly spread about rapists, murderers, and "armed youth gangs" looting and terrorizing the facility. Vending machines around the arena had been smashed and looted, and crack vials littered the restroom. Blankets and sheets were in short supply. Families slept on sheets of cardboard and covered themselves with vinyl ripped from the sides of the stadium. One man jumped off of the rafters to commit suicide. Officials later confirmed that he had just found out his home had been destroyed. One drug addict overdosed and died, while four other people died of natural causes. Meanwhile, countless others suffered as witnesses to each other's agony. Gordon Russell of the *New Orleans Times-Picayune* called it "a scene from the Apocalypse." Some were angry that Mayor Ray Nagin had not yet stopped in to address evacuees, as Blanco had done on Tuesday. Flown in by helicopter, she met agitated New Orleans residents face-to-face and quickly spoke out publicly against the conditions she had witnessed firsthand. She ordered an evacuation of the facility but set no timetable for doing so.

Still, as bad as things were inside the Superdome, they were even worse inside the flooded city, where people seeking safety waded through the floodwaters with shell-shocked eyes. Those who could not manage on their own were placed on wooden planks that became floating gurneys for the sick, the elderly, and the disabled. The water people found themselves trudging through was a nasty combination of oil, debris, and bacteria-infested liquid that spewed from open sewer pipes. Some reported seeing snakes, fish, and even snapping turtles, while mosquitoes that had been drawn to the massive plot of stagnant water raised fears that people might catch West Nile Virus or other diseases. Fortunately, many of these fears about disease and toxins were not realized. There was no major West Nile virus outbreak, and the level of dangerous carcinogens proved to be about the same as typical storm water runoff, according to a study conducted by a Louisiana State University environmental engineer. In terms of sheer horror, though, nothing could compare to the sight of a dead body floating to the water's surface. Waterlogged corpses were found floating across the city or washed up on the edges of dry land, as much a public spectacle as animals killed alongside an interstate.

Confusion reigned at the city's emergency hotlines. All 120 of the city's "911" operators abandoned their police headquarters due to the flooding, and calls were redirected to the fire department in their absence. Unfortunately, the fire station had also been evacuated, so the state police emergency headquarters in Baton Rouge found itself picking up the slack. As waters rose, so did the number of calls coming into Baton Rouge. Immediately following Katrina, the state police received 467 calls. But on Tuesday, that number multiplied to 1,875, according to the *Washington Post*. By Wednesday and Thursday, the total number of incoming calls was up to 3,108 and then 3,284. As *Post* reporter Ceci Connolly pointed out on November 8, "What was strange was not the volume of calls or that they were made, but how they ended up so far away from people who needed help."

Just as law and order deteriorated inside the Superdome, the flooded city became a free-for-all of looting and lawlessness. For evidence of just how crazy things had gotten, a person had to look no further than the Wal-Mart store on Tchoupitoulas Street, where people eagerly loaded shopping carts with clothing, gadgets, and any other merchandise they could get their hands on. When MSNBC sent a camera crew out to film the mayhem, they found the police in the most unlikely of places—Aisle Three. That is where the journalists found two officers "shopping" for some free shoes. *New Orleans Times-Picayune* staffers reported seeing one officer walk out of the store with hands full of DVDs and another load up a shopping cart with a compact computer and a 27-inch flat-screen television. When the city needed them most, many police officers simply neglected their duties. An estimated 200 of New Orleans's 1,600 police officers failed to show up for duty, according to statements later made by Deputy Police Superintendent Warren Riley.

While some of the officers were busy trying to track down missing family members, others "simply left because they could not deal with the catastrophe." Tragically, two

Signs like the one in this photo were seen on businesses all over New Orleans as residents began looting stores and homes. Many took only food and water, while others (including some police officers), stole electronics, clothes, and other things of value.

officers killed themselves shortly after the storm. Some fled to nearby cities such as Houston, where New Orleans police vehicles were regularly seen driving around town. A local hotel owner reported that a group of eight officers who were staying there went on a drinking and stealing binge for several nights. They took "everything from Adidas shoes to Rolex watches," according to information reported on CNN. Some officers used Katrina as an excuse to drive several brand-new Cadillacs off of a major downtown car lot. This was an especially creative interpretation of the city's directive to utilize any resources "necessary to cope with the local disaster emergency."

Granted, the officers who stayed had an increasingly difficult and dangerous job. At first, they had been ordered to venture into the waters to help save people stranded in their homes. By Wednesday, however, they were instructed to focus entirely on looters and other lawbreakers. Wal-Mart's entire gun selection had been raided, and armed bandits were said to be roaming the streets. One officer was shot in the head trying to protect a store, and though the officer lived, looting continued. Garbage cans and inflatable mattresses became transport vehicles for TV sets, DVD players, and other electronic equipment. A forklift was used to smash through a pharmacy's windows. One bus driver who was transporting nursing home residents reported his vehicle being hijacked, while the governor's office reported a group of people trying to break into the Children's Hospital. Even more unbelievably, there were reports of people shooting at Coast Guard rescue choppers!

Thanks to relentless coverage from television news networks, the whole country got to see New Orleans's lawlessness firsthand. By Thursday, Governor Blanco appeared on TV with a serious warning. She said that the National Guard troops stationed around the city "have M-16s and they are locked and loaded. These troops know how to shoot to kill . . . and I expect they will."

It is one thing when such tough talk is directed at actual thugs or looters. But there was a fine line between criminal looting and simply foraging for food, water, and other supplies needed for survival. Case in point: On Tuesday, police picked up a 73-year-old grandmother named Merlene Maten, who they accused of stealing $63.50 worth of items from a neighborhood convenience store. Maten insisted that she was merely getting a sausage from a cooler in the trunk of her car when police nabbed her at a spot near the store and threw her in jail. She stayed there for 16 days, but after a large national senior citizens' advocacy group, FEMA attorneys, a private lawyer, and even the convenience store owner herself, pleaded that she should be let go, Maten's charges were eventually dropped, just like they were in 84 of 189 other looting cases in Jefferson Parish. The district attorney had decided to forgo cases in which people were stealing for survival rather than luxury.

WHERE ARE THE FEDS?

With the Superdome growing increasingly tense and New Orleans descending into lawlessness, it was clear that local and state resources were not going to be enough. FEMA had continually promised to provide ice, food, water, and medicine to victims, as well as buses to help lead them to safety. But as Wednesday turned into Thursday, there was no sign of any of these things. Where were the Feds?

It's interesting that so much of the Bush administration's attention had been focused on the Middle East—especially ever since the United States declared war on Iraq in 2003. Fighting in that country had brought about a humanitarian crisis that required U.S. military troops, National Guard officers, food, water, and other supplies. This is exactly what America needed now, two years later, in the city of New Orleans. But with 35 percent of Louisiana's National Guard troops having been shipped off to help the efforts in Iraq, President Bush and his closest advisers were left open to charges that they had forgotten about America's interests at home while trying to fulfill their agenda abroad. Katrina was more than a challenge, it was a test. And how well Bush's Department of Homeland Security and FEMA performed on this test would play a major role in shaping Bush's legacy as a president.

6 No Help in Sight

It had been two days since Cory Delany first tried flagging down helicopters from his aunt's rooftop, and so far, none had extended a rescue basket. "They would just give us a thumbs-up and keep going," he told *City Pages*. It was not so much that Cory was worried about himself as he was concerned about his mom. Bound to her wheelchair, she grew weaker and more tired with each passing hour. Delany figured that the best way to help his family find safety was to build a raft. So, along with his uncle, he went outside to gather plywood. But just as the two men were putting the finishing touches on their homemade flotation device, an actual rescue boat pulled up. The family piled in.

The boat took them to a landing area, where they were greeted by an officer with an M16 machine gun. He told them to head toward the interstate, where evacuees were to be picked up by rescue buses, presumably provided by FEMA. "We had to walk like four miles, pulling my mama 'cause she didn't have no foot pedals on her wheelchair," Delany remembered, telling his story to *City Pages*. "They was out in the water somewhere. By that time her neck wasn't moving too much and she wasn't too responsive."

Along with 2,000 hungry and bedraggled evacuees, the Delanys waited out on the Interstate, a secondary drop-off point for rescued New Orleanians, where the number of citizens was growing by the hour. Beginning at 10:00 A.M., bus after bus would drive past the desperate masses of people who had gathered there—the sick, the elderly, and mothers tending to small children. It came across like a cruel tease. Each time a bus would drive by, the people would huddle up to it, hoping this would finally be their ticket out of the city. But the buses never stopped. They just kept driving. This continued for hours, well into nightfall.

The Delanys ended up waiting for three days alongside the other roadside victims. Most of them were African American, and the fact that media outlets had taken to calling them

New Orleans residents sit on highway overpasses, above the floodwaters, waiting for news of evacuation. Despite promises of local officials to send buses to transport citizens to places with bearable living conditions, many people waited a week before any buses appeared.

"refugees," did not sit well with several prominent black leaders, including the civil rights activist Al Sharpton and Bruce Gordon, president of the National Association for the Advancement of Colored People. "These people are fellow Americans," Gordon told reporters. "Using the word refugees makes it sound like they are not of us."

Of course, the storm evacuees were Americans. But they were not being treated as such. They had been denied the most basic elements of disaster relief—namely, instructions on where to go to find long-term shelter, safety, and running water. At the Superdome, they had been treated more like criminals than victims by some overly aggressive troops from the National Guard. Worst of all, they had been told repeatedly by President Bush and FEMA Director Michael Brown that help was coming, but by Thursday, it had yet to arrive.

As media outlets covered this hard-to-believe story, race emerged as a prevailing theme. Speaking off-the-cuff during one CNN broadcast, the TV newscaster Wolf Blitzer casually noted "You simply get chills every time you see these poor individuals. So many of these people, almost all of them that we see, are so poor and *they are so black*, and this is going to raise lots of questions for people who are watching this story unfold." Not exactly worded eloquently, Blitzer's comments nonetheless underscored a question that was on the minds of many who watched the story from New Orleans unfold: Was race a factor in the slow federal response?

Appearing later in the week on a CBS Sunday news program, the actress and humorist Nancy Giles offered her own answer: "If the majority of the hardest hit victims of Hurricane Katrina in New Orleans were white people, they would not have gone for days without food and water, forcing many to steal for mere survival. Their bodies would not have been left to float in putrid water."

As New Orleans's victims waited for federal help to arrive, the city's local officials and National Guardsmen

Finding Fats Domino

After Katrina's floodwaters immersed New Orleans's Lower Ninth Ward, music fans waited nervously for days to hear what had become of Fats Domino, the 77-year-old rock-and-roll icon who lived in the neighborhood in a modest but flashy three-story, pink-roofed house. News outlets reported that Domino was missing, and it was not until Thursday, when his daughter recognized him in a photo of a rescue boat that had run days earlier in the *New Orleans Times-Picayune*, that any-one had reason to believe he may have survived.

Domino was picked up by rescue workers Monday evening and was flown by helicopter to a shelter in Baton Rouge. Since his home was filled with 15 feet of floodwater, Domino, two of his daughters, and a son-in-law found themselves staying in Baton Rouge with a distant family friend, Louisiana State University quarterback JaMarcus Russell. Appropriately enough, Domino had been working on a new album prior to the hurricane. Its title?—*Alive and Kickin'*.

Domino decided to donate the album's proceeds to the Tipitina's Foundation, an organization dedicated to preserving New Orleans's musical culture.

found themselves trying to manage yet another crisis. The city's Ernest N. Morial Convention Center, a facility normally used to host business conventions, was now teeming with more than 20,000 storm survivors—about as many as there were at the Superdome.

City officials entertained the idea of opening the three-story facility for use as a temporary shelter early Tuesday. By the time evening rolled around, they did not have a choice. Anticipating that the convention center would open, a group of evacuees had gathered outside the building, which spanned 11 city blocks. Growing increasingly impatient, somebody smashed a chair through the facility's glass front door. Over the next few days, people poured in by the thousands.

Few of them could have been sadder than Allie Harris. Along with her husband, Booker, the 93-year-old woman had been loaded onto the back of a Ryder truck by rescuers who had picked her up at her flooded eastern New Orleans home. But when she and her husband debarked at the convention center, only one of them was alive. Booker had died in transit.

Rescue workers evidently had more important things to do than take a body down to the coroner's office or mortuary, so, they simply covered the 91-year-old man in a yellow quilt and left him to rest in the hot sun. Booker Harris was exposed for two days to children and their families staying at the convention center. No matter where people found themselves in New Orleans—at the convention center, the Superdome, or along the hot interstate—living or dead, they had to wait for help all the same.

For the next few days, the National Guard did its best to maintain order. Evacuees sprawled among the filth on blankets, pillows, or inflatable mattresses in the building's lobby, while squatters used hallways as toilets. Rumors of rapists and killers spread as quickly as a storm surge. Looters raided the kitchen of beer and liquor, and somebody accidentally started a fire while trying to cook. The building's lobby, which was where most people camped, quickly became a junkyard of trash and human waste. By Friday, it had been five days since the storm—five days without a bath, shower, tooth-brushing, clean clothes, or a safe place to stay.

Back in Baton Rouge, rumors about riots and looting in the city's downtown had begun making their way around town Thursday. Within hours, people were making a run to one of the city's biggest gun stores. Crowds lined up in the parking lot waiting to get in. Another area gun supplier reported selling 170 firearms in the three days after Katrina, though he did point out that he refused to sell to two men who "seemed too upset, too hot-headed about the influx of people to the city," according to the September 15 *Advocate*.

"ALL THE PERSPECTIVE YOU NEED"

For seasoned news reporters, many of whom had covered wars in foreign countries and bigger natural disasters such as the 2004 Asian tsunami, the disarray that had overcome New Orleans was especially shocking. Outside of the convention center, the body of yet another dead man, this one killed by gunfire, lay outside on a grassy median. Reporting live for CNN, anchor Soledad O'Brien pointed out that only by Saturday did somebody at least have the decency to cover it up with a comforter. "At some point they'll figure it out and move it off," she said, her dismay hardly concealed.

Shepard Smith, a Fox News correspondent who had been in New Orleans covering the crisis all week, reported one of the most memorable news segments of the disaster Friday evening. Appearing on the popular talk show *Hannity and Colmes*, he was asked by one of the cohosts to provide a Katrina update. Looking worn-out and thoroughly disenchanted, he was almost at a loss for words. "It's one of the first stories I've ever covered where questions as simple as 'why do people on the easily accessible bridge not get food and water and don't even get instructions on where to go to get food and water and medical attention,'" he said. "It's the first time I've not known the answer to that and I'm not sure there is an answer." There were plenty of food and rescue workers in town, Smith added, but also plenty of starving evacuees. Nothing made sense, and he refused to try to make sense of it. Journalists are typically expected to remain composed and objective as they report a story to their television audience, but Smith was not even going to try to pretend that he did not have an opinion on the situation. He was disgusted, dismayed, and eager to tell the world exactly what was on his mind.

The show's producers quickly cut to Geraldo Rivera, who was reporting live from the convention center. But if they were expecting a more balanced counterpoint, they were sorely disappointed. Rivera was even more visibly unsettled. Pacing in front of the garbage-strewn dome, he asserted angrily, "Sean, I can't emphasize what Shep just said enough. He said it exactly right. There is no earthly answer that anyone can understand why these people after six days are still in this filthy, filthy miserable convention center. Why are they still here?" Pointing to a freeway within walking distance of the building, he continued: "I'll tell you what I would have done and what I would still do. I would say let them walk out of here. Let them walk away from the filth. Let them walk away from the devastation." Tears welling up in his eyes, Rivera picked up a 15-month-old baby. "You see there are so many babies here," he said, his voice straining under the weight of his sadness.

The camera cut back to Smith, who had even more discouraging news. People *had* tried to walk across the freeway and bridge out of town. The problem was, when they got to the end of the bridge that led into Gretna, the small Jefferson Parish town just outside of New Orleans, armed sheriff's deputies were telling them to turn around! Rather than embrace the Katrina victims with open arms and generosity, Gretna officials instead pulled out their guns and ordered evacuees to turn around. Reports of violence and looting had been rampant, and they did not want a replay of New Orleans's problems in their own small town.

Cohost Sean Hannity, smooth, unemotional, and never failing to appear anything but confident and polished, asked Smith for a little more "perspective" on the situation—a more subtle way of telling his reporter to quit harping on the negative. But no sooner was that word out of Hannity's mouth than

Smith interjected wildly. "That is perspective! That is all the perspective you need!"

PROMISES, PROMISES

By Wednesday, August 31, FEMA had worked with Blanco's office to come up with a plan to bus people out of the Superdome to Houston, Texas, where they would stay at a Red Cross shelter established at the Houston Astrodome. That afternoon, President Bush announced that FEMA would also be distributing meals, water, tarps, ice, generators, blankets, and cots to victims. But by Thursday, these things had yet to surface, and FEMA had only shuffled a few-dozen busloads of people to Houston, their plan halted after they had received reports of the Coast Guard's helicopters being shot at and fires intentionally being lit in the way of oncoming buses.

That morning, the ABC network's Diane Sawyer, host of the popular program *Good Morning America*, interviewed Bush about the slow federal response. True to what had become his form for the Katrina disaster, Bush was nothing but reassuring. He said that a "major transportation lift" was on its way to the Superdome, along with food, water, and supplies. He also offered his opinion that he did not think "anybody anticipated the breach of the levees" and all the while said nothing about the convention center. Neither did Homeland Security Chief Michael Chertoff when he gave a press conference that afternoon. It was bizarre that the federal government's top-ranking officials were not only failing to respond to the situation at the convention center—they were not mentioning it at all. A National Public Radio broadcaster asked Chertoff about the people stranded at the convention center that evening, and the Homeland Security Chief suggested that reports of evacuees being housed there were just rumors. Was it possible that Bush and Chertoff had no idea people were even stranded there?

When NBC's Brian Williams spoke to FEMA's Michael Brown, he asked him why the agency was not air-dropping food into the convention center. Astonishingly, Brown admitted that "the federal government just learned about those people today." Failing to recognize that people were at the convention center was a major slipup, a public one no less—and according to later reports in the *New York Times*, President Bush was furious with both Brown and Chertoff.

In the days immediately following the disaster, Chertoff came across as always being a step behind the latest developments. Similar to his dismissal of convention center "rumors," he had scoffed at initial reports about the hurricane's damage but later confessed that this was only because newspaper

Superdome evacuees wait in line for buses to take them to the Houston Astrodome. Officials told residents that buses were on their way to take them to safer locations, but miscommunication and disorganization resulted in people waiting for days before the buses finally arrived to rescue them.

headlines had led him to believe that the worst expected of New Orleans had come to pass (clearly, he was not reading the *New Orleans Times-Picayune*). A fellow FEMA staffer seemed similarly oblivious to the peril striking New Orleans Tuesday afternoon. At a press conference in Baton Rouge, FEMA coordinator Bill Lokey said, "I don't want to alarm everybody that, you know, New Orleans is filling up like a bowl. That's just not happening."

Journalists pummeled Brown. "How is it possible that we're getting better intel [intelligence] than you're getting?" CNN anchor Soledad O'Brien asked him on CNN, referring to the situation at the convention center. "We had a crew in the air. We were showing live pictures of the people." *Nightline* host Ted Koppel was similarly baffled. "Don't you guys watch television? Don't you listen to the radio?" he asked.

While Homeland Security and FEMA suffered from evident lapses in communication, Bush and his highest-ranking advisers seemed to be acting almost nonchalant about the disaster. With waters rising on Wednesday, Vice President Dick Cheney continued vacationing in Wyoming, while Secretary of State Condoleezza Rice spent her day in New York City shopping for shoes and her evening at a performance of the Broadway play *Spamalot*, where she was booed. President Bush did not even fly into New Orleans to address Katrina victims in person, as he did three days after the terror attacks of 9/11. Instead, he flew over the city in the presidential jet Air Force One, surveying the destruction from miles above.

FLASHBACK: HURRICANE BETSY

Many have contrasted Bush's reaction to Hurricane Katrina with the behavior of another president, Lyndon Johnson, who had to weather the fallout from Hurricane Betsy. Almost immediately after Betsy struck, President Johnson rounded up two Louisiana senators, five Congressmen, and a team of other administration officials to fly down to New Orleans on Air Force One. "I am here because I want to see with my own eyes what the unhappy alliance of wind and water have done to this land and its people," Johnson told a small crowd that had gathered to greet him at the Louisiana airport. "And when I leave today to go back to Washington, you can be sure that the federal government's total resources will be turned to Louisiana to help the state and its citizens find its way back from this tragedy."

Flashlight in hand, Johnson toured the dark and powerless city. He marched into the George Washington grade school, where hundreds of weather-worn victims ate scraps of tinned meat or raw carrots and slept on classroom desks. Recognizing their president in the dim glow of a portable light, some flood victims cried out in frustration. "We must have clean water," one person shouted. Another sobbed that she had not had anything to eat or drink in 12 hours. For those who were already restless and unnerved by the fact that their homes, cars, and family heirlooms had all been destroyed, the added stress of hunger and thirst was almost unbearable.

Like a drill sergeant, Johnson took command of the situation, ordering his director of emergency planning to do "everything possible" to help storm survivors. He told the mayor to open the city's warehouses and bring soft drinks to those without access to clean water. The urgency of Johnson's response came out of his own concern for victims, as well as pressures applied by Louisiana's state and congressional leaders. One of the president's spokesman told reporters that Johnson had talked with Louisiana politicians nonstop for two hours after the storm hit New Orleans.

Such open lines of communication between city, state, and federal government agencies may have been all that was needed to persuade George Bush to respond sooner to the devastation wrought by Katrina. Or, perhaps Bush did not intuitively recognize the severity of the problem before him, while his predecessor Johnson did. Regardless, as flood images saturated online and broadcast media for days, Bush had no excuse for not being attuned to the situation. When he declared to Diane Sawyer that he understood "the anxiety of people on the ground. I can imagine—I just can't imagine what it is like to be waving a sign saying 'come and get me now,'" it did not come across as very convincing to many.

Bush did not meet directly with bedraggled storm survivors. He did not hear the cries of those still needing to be rescued from their homes or witness firsthand the vicious behavior of a traumatized dog, left without its owner in the unfamiliar circumstances of a flood-stricken roadside. He did not smell the unforgettable stench of death or feel the tremors of anger ricocheting across the convention center and Superdome as storm survivors fended for themselves. Granted, it was not his responsibility to single-handedly save survivors. That duty fell largely on local officials and his Department of Homeland Security, which seemed to be dragging its feet.

ALL EYES ON FEMA

By Thursday evening, Mayor Ray Nagin was feeling tired, overwhelmed, and a little bit helpless. His city's resources had been stretched thin, and it was still anybody's guess how many citizens would make it out alive. The city's chief of emergency operations, Terry Ebbert, was publicly bad-mouthing FEMA, calling the agency's failure to establish control of the situation a "national disgrace." Bush and Chertoff had continually pledged to the mayor that resources (including four U.S. Navy ships) would be arriving throughout the week, but Nagin was tired of promises. He wanted to see ships, National Guard troops, buses, food, ice, water, and all of the other things needed to take control of the situation, for himself. Enough was enough.

The mayor was so frustrated that he called in to a local radio station Thursday evening. Appearing live on the *Garland Robinette Show*, a popular local news and commentary program, Nagin went off on a tirade of criticism directed toward President Bush and the federal government. "Where's the beef?" the mayor asked, demanding to see the federal help that had been promised.

"Don't tell me 40,000 people are coming here," he continued, referring to an earlier request for more National Guard troops made by Governor Blanco. "They're not here. It's too doggone late," he said. He ended the interview with a simple suggestion for Bush, Brown, Chertoff, and other federal officials. Unable to refrain from using expletives, Nagin passionately implored the government to "do something, and let's fix the biggest . . . crisis in the history of this country." The mayor had finally articulated what many newscasters and ordinary citizens were already saying, albeit a bit less politely.

7 Exodus from the Gulf Coast

As timing would have it, the federal response picked up dramatically after Nagin's scolding. Thousands of National Guard troops arrived in New Orleans on Friday, September 2, and many of them headed for the Ernest N. Morial Convention Center to pass out food and water. Some evacuees were grateful for these basic supplies, but others were upset because there were still no buses (as Geraldo Rivera pointed out later that evening). At the Superdome, FEMA buses made a little bit of headway, picking up survivors who had to wade through trash up to their knees. Local hospitals began shuffling out doctors, nurses, patients, and evacuees who had holed up there. New Orleans Charity Hospital evacuated 2,200 people, including 363 patients, while Louisiana State University hospital shipped out 110 patients and 490 others.

That day, President Bush finally arrived in the Gulf Coast to tour affected areas in Mississippi, Alabama, and Louisiana. In New Orleans, he met with Blanco, Brown, Chertoff, and Nagin, who, despite having criticized the president's "flyover" of the city on Air Force One, ended up taking a long shower on the grounded presidential jet. It must have been awkward for the mayor and president to meet eye-to-eye just a day after Nagin had skewered Bush on the radio. But the leaders managed to put differences aside, and they worked to finally come up with a solution to the problem that had been hampering relief efforts all week—they came up with a strategy that stated definitively who was in control of Louisiana's National Guard forces. According to Nagin, the governor, president,

President Bush (*right*), Louisiana Governor Kathleen Blanco (*center*), and Homeland Security Secretary Michael Chertoff (*behind Blanco*) met with the Louisiana National Guard to discuss strategies of rescue and recovery for the city. The failure to respond to the crisis of Katrina was partly due to a lack in communications between federal and local officials, who received harsh criticism from the public.

and FEMA had not, thus far, been on the same page. Over the weekend, FEMA would begin evacuating people en masse, taking them to the Houston, Texas, Astrodome or to Red Cross shelters across the country.

If the president had any doubts about Michael Brown's performance, he did not reveal them publicly. "Brownie, you're doing a heck of a job," Bush told the FEMA director at a news conference in Mobile, Alabama. It was a phrase that came back to haunt him, echoed in countless newspapers, magazines, television shows, and Web sites—the phrase that came to epitomize, more than anything, people's perceptions that Bush had been oblivious to the disaster all along. Appearing in a blue, button-down shirt, sleeves rolled up like a man hard at work, Bush continued speaking with the "can-do" optimism that marked every one of his public appearances in regards to the disaster. "The good news is—and it's hard for some to see it now—that out of this chaos is going to come a fantastic Gulf Coast, like it was before. Out of the rubbles of Trent Lott's house—he's lost his entire house—there's going to be a fantastic house. And I'm looking forward to sitting on the porch." Bush was speaking about a powerful Mississippi senator whose money and influence far exceeded the majority of Katrina victims.

Such unwavering optimism struck a sour note with many Katrina survivors. It was one thing to think positively—that is certainly a quality that most people want in a leader. But there is also an expectation of compassion and empathy. Many criticized Bush for not failing to recognize how truly horrible the situation was for Gulf Coast residents. People had lost everything they had. In Biloxi, Mississippi, for example, one man told CNN that all that was left of his house and belongings was a single shoe. In nearby Waveland, only tiny reminders of the lives people once led could be found among the wreckage—things such as "family photos, Barbie dolls, jazz records, whiskey bottles," according to one CBS News report.

Kanye's Revenge

Quotations often come to symbolize a particular time period or event—like when Martin Luther King declared "I have a dream" during the civil rights era, or when Neil Armstrong famously stated that the U.S. Moon landing was "one small step for man; one giant leap for mankind." Hurricane Katrina has no shortage of memorable quotations, but none sparked as much controversy as the statement that rapper Kanye West made in front of millions of viewers during a live television appearance on NBC's "Concert for Hurricane Relief" the evening of Friday, September 2. Abandoning his script, West told Americans who had tuned in to the broadcast that "George Bush doesn't care about black people."

This was definitely not what NBC had bargained for when it booked the musician to help solicit funds for the Katrina rescue efforts. West was supposed to say a few things about the devastation and rebuilding, but instead began his impromptu remarks with complaints about the slow federal response and media portrayals of African-American evacuees as criminals or "looters." NBC removed his comments from its taped West Coast broadcast, but celebrities including fellow rapper and music producer Sean "Diddy" Combs applauded West for saying publicly what others were thinking privately. Others, including former congressman and conservative commentator Newt Gingrich, felt the rapper's remarks were "despicable and dishonest." But, they grabbed attention nonetheless. People began selling t-shirts with the slogan, while one musician even recorded a song inspired by it.

Could Bush really relate to what it was like to have an entire life's savings or possessions wiped out by the storm? And did he understand that "Brownie" as he called the FEMA director, was hardly doing a "heck of a job." Michael Brown had dropped the ball, just like his boss Michael Chertoff.

Nevertheless, under the leadership of the National Guard's General Russell Honore, a native Louisianan who had already begun barking some orders in New Orleans on Wednesday, massive evacuations and relief occurred over the weekend. The airport filled up from wall to wall with evacuees, who were flown off to temporary shelters all around the country. Appearing Monday at the Astrodome in Houston, the former first lady Barbara Bush added yet another unfortunate gaffe to the series of embarrassing public statements made after Katrina. Touring the facility with her husband, former president George H.W. Bush and former president Bill Clinton, the mother to the current president claimed that the setup was favorable for evacuees. "So many of the people in the arena here, you know, were underprivileged anyway, so this is working very well for them," she chuckled.

The more financially well-off of the Katrina evacuees tried to find housing in areas close to the affected Gulf Coast regions, such as Baton Rouge, where all available real estate and rental housing was quickly purchased. True to the laws of supply and demand, real estate prices went up in unaffected areas near the Gulf region in the months after Katrina. Victims found housing with people all over the country who opened their houses to total strangers left homeless by the flood. Web sites such as Hurricanehousing.net and Craigslist.com helped connect victims with people willing to put them up for a few days, weeks, or months.

Those who had taken refuge at the Superdome and convention center were shuffled to cities all over the United States—from Salt Lake City, Utah; to Pensacola, Florida; to Minneapolis, Minnesota, where Cory Delany's family resettled.

Federal Emergency Management Agency (FEMA) director Michael Brown became the scapegoat as efforts to send aid to the Gulf Coast failed to help hurricane victims. Later, as media interviews and exposed e-mails revealed his oblivious and glib attitude, the shamed Brown resigned as FEMA head.

Through various nonprofit and government programs, they found housing in various hotels or apartment buildings set up for evacuees. For many, it was like starting life anew. The world they once knew had been destroyed in the flood. Sadly, as many were making their farewell trips out of the city over the weekend, law and order continued spiraling out of control. Police got into a shootout with a group of men on Danziger bridge, wounding four and killing two, including an unarmed mentally retarded man. Four officers were charged with murder and attempted murder in connection to the case, while three other officers were charged with attempted murder.

OUTPOURING OF GENEROSITY

One of the positive things to come out of the Katrina tragedy was the outpouring of generosity from all over the world. More than $4 billion was raised to assist the rebuilding of the Gulf Coast, through major events like NBC's fundraising telethon to a child's lemonade stand in Houston, which raised $1,000 in two days. Most of the money raised for Katrina efforts went to the American Red Cross, although hundreds of lesser-known charities also rushed in to claim their share of Katrina donations.

With that kind of money floating around, there were bound to be problems, however, and an unintended consequence of post-Katrina generosity was a corresponding rise in tragedy-related scams. Just as scam artists hustled to make money off of well-meaning donors after the 9/11 attacks, they did the same after Katrina. They used Web sites that appeared to be linked to charitable donations but were actually just a way for criminals to extract money from people's credit cards online. Others posed as Katrina victims themselves.

Back in New Orleans, the process of picking up the devastation was only beginning. Rescue teams charged with inspecting houses came up with a system for identifying what they found inside. It involved spray-painting an "X" on the

After the waters receded, officials began to shift their focus from rescue to recovery. Here, the markings painted on the house indicate who searched the house, when, and the grim findings inside.

side of the house and filling in each of the "X" quadrants with identifying information including the date the building was searched, the number of hazards found inside, and the initials of the team that performed the inspection—NJLETF for New Jersey Law Enforcement Task Force, for example. The most significant of all the markings was also the most disturbing. The number scribbled into the bottom quadrant represented the number of dead bodies found inside.

Walking through the neighborhoods that once were the Lower Ninth Ward or Gentilly, hundreds of these "X's" could be seen scrawled upon the splintered homes. The most unsettling parts of any story are usually those left unspoken, and every red or black numeral sprayed at the bottom of one of those "X's" told a story, each a tragedy, scrawled like graffiti in the decaying city that once was New Orleans. It was chilling.

As rescuers canvased parts of the city that had been previously inaccessible due to the floodwaters, they made even

New Orleans Animal Rescue

After Katrina, animal welfare experts braced themselves for the biggest animal rescue operation in history. An estimated 250,000 pets were left stranded during the storm—from dogs and cats to parrots and fish, according to the PBS special "Katrina's Animal Rescue." Rescuers saved at least 15,000 in the ensuing weeks, many of them in a pitiful state of health. They were often hungry, dehydrated, covered in sores, and suffering from bacterial infections and other ailments that left them on the verge of death.

Animals were traumatized by Katrina in much the same way that humans were. Dogs, cats, and other domestic animals who survived the storm became anxious or even vicious at the sound of heavy winds, rain, or rushing water, according to Nick Dodman, an animal expert quoted by PBS. Dodman suggested that pet owners who want to help animals recover should get them back into regular feeding and walking routines, set up comfortable play areas, and provide plenty of loving attention.

For those pet owners who live in disaster-prone areas, Dodman suggested preparing ahead of time to make sure animals can fend for themselves during tense situations. This can be as simple as leaving out fresh water and food. "A little bit of forethought can go a long way," he said.

more grim discoveries. On September 12, a state health official announced that the bodies of 45 hospital patients, most of them terminally ill, had been recovered at the Memorial Medical Center in Uptown New Orleans. When investigators began questioning the hospital's staffers about what had happened there in the days immediately following the flood, the story grew even more shocking. With no water or electricity, doctors and nurses found it exceedingly difficult to care for patients inside the sweltering hot facility. Some began discussing euthanasia, or mercy killings. One doctor told CNN that he was in a second-floor triage area where everyone was cleared except for patients, a hospital administrator, and two doctors. One of them had a handful of syringes.

An investigation revealed that four of the victims were found to have a lethal drug combination in their systems, although the coroner declined to classify their cause of death as a homicide. A special grand jury called to examine the evidence chose not to indict the doctor, who said she only administered medication to alleviate patients' pain. Charges against the two nurses were eventually dropped.

A PROMISE TO REBUILD

On September 15, with parts of the city still submerged and the 82nd Airborne Division on patrol, Bush made a dramatic appearance at Jackson Square in New Orleans. In an address to the nation, he promised to do everything possible to rebuild the Gulf Coast and said that it was the duty of all Americans to confront a deeper, more persistent problem—the problem of poverty, which led so many people to find themselves flooded out of their homes to begin with. People with money generally did not live in low-lying neighborhoods. And they had the means to evacuate when necessary. Whether history will remember Bush as a president who confronted poverty remains to be seen, and is highly doubtful, yet Bush's speech contained a few lines that placed Katrina in the context of all of America's great disasters and provided some hope for the future. Speaking behind a floodlit podium, he declared,

> In the life of this nation, we have often been reminded that nature is an awesome force, and that all life is fragile. We're the heirs of men and women who lived through those first terrible winters at Jamestown and Plymouth, who rebuilt Chicago after a great fire, and San Francisco after a great earthquake, who reclaimed the prairie from the Dust Bowl of the 1930s. Every time, the people of this land have come back from fire, flood, and storm to build anew—and to build better than what we had before. Americans have never left our destiny to the whims of nature—and we will not start now.

8 Rebuilding Lives and Homes

Just weeks into the disaster, Michael Brown called it quits on September 12. It had been especially hard for the director of FEMA, who had become a scapegoat for all of the things that went wrong in the disaster response—things that were within his control as well as things that were outside of it. Many questioned Brown's credentials, which included an 11-year stint as the Judges and Stewards Commissioner for the International Arabian Horse Association.

Brown defended himself in a speech he later gave to a group of graduate students, claiming that Republican Bush administration officials chose not to take control of the situation in Louisiana in order to embarrass Blanco, a Democrat. It was a cynical observation that a White House spokesman denied, but it spoke to the bigger issue of politics as they relate to natural disasters. As Katrina proved, disasters are not the time to play politics and to work out personal grudges.

FACT VS. FICTION

The disaster also provided lessons for the news media and the civic leaders who occasionally rely upon it for information. In tense situations, it is easy for rumors to get out of hand. And that is exactly what happened in New Orleans in the days following the storm. Rumors of rape and gunplay at the convention center and Superdome proved to be largely unfounded. One doctor reportedly rolled a refrigerated 18-wheeler over to the Superdome in order to collect what had been reported to him as 200 dead bodies. The actual total was six. Despite reports of bodies being piled up at the convention center, only four were actually recovered.

Accounts of people shooting at rescue helicopters also seem to have been exaggerated. While one man was charged for doing this, it seemed to be an isolated incident. Some have suggested that any other shots fired into the air when rescues were being conducted were merely attempts to capture rescuers' attention. Without these reports, there may not have been such a rush among people in Baton Rouge, New Orleans, and other affected communities to arm themselves with guns. The officials who pushed back New Orleans evacuees arriving in Gretna may have acted with less hostility.

WHAT'S NEXT?

Even the most current statistics do not tell the full story of the Katrina disaster, the legacy of which will go on for decades. While the floodwaters may have dried, the storm continues to affect survivors in different ways. Battles between residents and their insurance companies have been waged inside of courtrooms. Property damages are continually being reassessed. The cost of repairing the levees alone is estimated to be about $10 billion. And even though Katrina was said to have killed more than 1,600 people, more people continue to die from Katrina-related injuries, sometimes from causes that are not so obvious.

Take Sylvester Major. The 59-year-old former laundry worker spent his entire life in New Orleans and escaped from the flood unharmed. He even endured the misery of the convention center. Still, when Major died a year later, his family

In the wake of Katrina, volunteers came from across the United States to help in any way possible. Former President Jimmy Carter (*above*) joins the effort to rebuild the Gulf Coast with Habitat for Humanity, an organization dedicated to building homes for those in need.

did not doubt for a second that the killer was Katrina. As one social worker explained to the Associated Press's Michael Roberts in an article appearing December 14, 2006, storm surges and falling trees were not the only causes of death among residents along the Gulf Coast. The depression and the trauma had taken a toll on his physical and mental health. "You really can die of a broken heart," explained Joann Powers, an employee of the Grace Living Centers nursing home. "I don't care what anyone says." Since so many residents evacuated to other parts of the country, it is difficult to say exactly how many people may have died prematurely, either because they were forced to go for days or weeks without proper medication or because the stress of the storm simply proved to be too much.

Two years after the storm, the New Orleans spirit has bounced back, and the unique traditions that made the city special continue to this day. Crowds gather on Bourbon Street in the French Quarter for the 2007 Mardi Gras celebration.

If you walked down Bourbon Street in New Orleans's once-bustling French Quarter a year after Katrina, you would not immediately think you were in what was once a disaster zone, save for the playfully sarcastic t-shirts: "Make levees, not war"; "I Stayed in New Orleans for Katrina and All I got Was This Lousy T-Shirt, a New Cadillac and a Plasma TV"; or "NOPD: Not our problem dude."

But clear on the other side of the city, the memories of Katrina were in plain sight, as some neighborhoods didn't look much different than they did after the floodwaters receded. As Mary Beth Romig, spokeswoman for the New Orleans Convention and Visitors Bureau explained to CNN, "We are a tale of two cities. We have a long way to go in those residential neighborhoods."

Many Katrina residents took shelter in temporary trailer communities set up by FEMA. Visiting these makeshift neighborhoods in December 2006, *New York Times* columnist Bob Herbert noted that their names were ironically pleasant: Mount Olive Gardens or Renaissance Village, to name just a few. Unfortunately, the reality of living in one of them was much more depressing. The "parks" were nothing more than "dusty, gravel-strewn lots filled with trailers that were designed to be hitched to cars for brief vacations or weekend getaways. The trailers, about 200 square feet each, were never meant to serve as homes for entire families." But that is exactly what they were up until their closure in November 2007.

After all the suffering endured at the hands of Katrina, it would be a tragedy if the city of New Orleans ultimately lost the people and the culture that made it unique. The question that now faces Mayor Ray Nagin and others concerned with preserving the once vibrant culture of New Orleans is this: Will the people come back? Without native New Orleanians—without the artists and musicians, the Cajuns and the Creoles, and all of the working-class people whose humor and charisma made New Orleans what it was, the city would cease to exist, or more likely, it would redevelop as something entirely different—a less culturally unique tourist town.

Nagin, like many die-hard New Orleanians, maintains a fierce optimism about his city's future. Speaking just weeks after the flood, he proudly declared that "I know New Orleanians, and once we're cooking the beignets [a French donut], once the gumbo is in the pot, and when red beans and rice are being served on Mondays in the city, they'll be back." Speaking on the television program *60 Minutes* a year later, he said the city would take five to seven years to rebuild, but that he had no doubt that it would recover, and that it would maintain the culture, the humor, and the people who made it so special.

Unfortunately, city, state, and federal leaders learned the hard way what happens if you ignore inevitable environmental problems. They learned why it is important to maintain

Despite losing so much in the flood, residents of the Gulf Coast are determined to return to their homes and rebuild their lives. A U.S. flag stands in front of a ruined house in Biloxi, Mississippi.

coastal wetlands (even in the face of pressure from businesses that might want to do otherwise). They learned why it is important to fund levees, floodwalls, and other elements needed for sound environmental engineering. Finally, they learned what could happen if the issue of global warming is not addressed.

Global warming will likely lead to more and more hurricanes like Katrina, more devastation, and more lost lives. While it is impossible to say for sure that global warming caused Katrina, studies have shown that global warming increases hurricane frequency and intensity. In this sense, we can learn from Katrina the consequences of ignoring this critical issue. Everyone has a responsibility to reduce the amount of electricity they use, the amount of gasoline they burn in automobiles, and to use environmentally friendly products in their household.

But these are all long-term objectives. In the shorter term, there are also things that can be done that can help minimize damage the next time a hurricane strikes a major city. First, better planning ahead of time can help save lives. If evacuation routes are designated and resources are dedicated to aid in the evacuation of people who cannot do so on their own, the amount of life lost to the storm can be reduced. Second, having the resources on hand to preempt a pending emergency can also make a difference. Some have argued that Louisiana National Guard officers could have sandbagged and built up levees in the days before the storm, a measure that may have prevented some flooding.

Ultimately, everyone can pay their respects to New Orleans not only by supporting charitable organizations but also by respecting the environment, actively working to fight poverty in their communities, and by becoming more civic-minded. In a democracy, the only way government will work for the people is if they get involved by voting and communicating with elected officials. That way the next time disaster strikes—days, months, or even years down the road, America will be ready.

Chronology

1927 Mississippi River flood

1965 Hurricane Betsy strikes New Orleans.

2005 **August 24:** Tropical Depression 12 strengthens into Tropical Storm Katrina over the central Bahamas, and a hurricane warning is issued for the southeastern Florida coast.

August 25: At 5:30 P.M., Hurricane Katrina strikes a coastal area near Miami as a Category 1 hurricane with winds of 130 kilometers per hour (80 mph).

Timeline

1965
Hurricane Betsy strikes New Orleans.

August 24, 2005
Tropical Depression 12 strengthens into Tropical Storm Katrina over the central Bahamas, and a hurricane warning is issued for the southeastern Florida coast.

August 25, 2005
At 5:30 P.M., Hurricane Katrina strikes a coastal area near Miami as a Category 1 hurricane with winds of 130 kilometers per hour (80 mph).

August 26, 2005
Katrina surfaces over the Gulf of Mexico. Louisiana governor Kathleen Blanco and Mississippi governor Haley Barbour declare states of emergency.

August 27, 2005
New Orleans mayor Ray Nagin announces a voluntary evacuation order and instructs "special-needs" residents to head to the Superdome.

August 28, 2005
At 10 A.M., the New Orleans mayor issues a mandatory evacuation order.

1965 **2005**

August 26: Katrina surfaces over the Gulf of Mexico. Louisiana governor Kathleen Blanco and Mississippi governor Haley Barbour declare states of emergency. By 10 P.M., the storm is on its way toward coastal Louisiana and Mississippi. Forecasters predict it will be Category 4 at landfall.

August 27: Around noon, New Orleans mayor Ray Nagin announces a voluntary evacuation order and instructs "special-needs" residents to head to the Superdome. President George W. Bush declares an emergency in Louisiana. The Department of Homeland Security and the Federal Emergency Management Agency (FEMA) are to coordinate all

August 29, 2005
At 6 A.M., Katrina hits east of New Orleans with 145-mph top-sustained winds; the U.S. Army Corps of Engineers receives reports of a 17th Street Canal breach. At 12:30 P.M., the Industrial Canal is breached and parts of the city begin to flood.

August 30, 2005
Mass flooding takes hold in neighborhoods, including the Lower Ninth Ward, Lakeview, Gentilly, and St. Bernard Parish.

August 31, 2005
President Bush holds a videoconference and views Katrina damage from Air Force One on his return to Washington.

September 2, 2005
At 8 A.M., National Guard troops arrive at the Superdome and the convention center to provide security and begin evacuations to shelters in other parts of the country.

September 12, 2005
Michael Brown resigns.

disaster relief efforts. National Hurricane Center director Max Mayfield calls Mayor Nagin at home in the evening to warn him to order an evacuation of New Orleans.

August 28: At 1 A.M., Katrina is a Category 4 storm; it is upgraded to Category 5 by 7 A.M. At 10 A.M., the New Orleans mayor issues a mandatory evacuation order.

August 29: At 6 A.M., Katrina hits east of New Orleans with 145-mph top-sustained winds; the U.S. Army Corps of Engineers receives reports of a 17th Street Canal breach. At 12:30 P.M., the Industrial Canal is breached and parts of the city begin to flood.

August 30: Mass flooding takes hold in neighborhoods, including the Lower Ninth Ward, Lakeview, Gentilly, and St. Bernard Parish. The Coast Guard and the Louisiana Department of Fish and Wildlife begin rescue operations. Mississippi governor Barbour says to FEMA Director Michael Brown, "I don't think you've seen anything like this. We're talking nuclear devastation."

August 31: FEMA serves 82,000 meals to people in the devastated area. 1,700 trucks are mobilized to supply ice, water, and supplies, but FEMA says it may take several days to reach victims due to bad roads. Superdome conditions are deplorable; evacuees who have gone to the Ernest N. Morial Convention Center face similar conditions. Bush holds a videoconference and views Katrina damage from Air Force One on his return to Washington.

September 1: FEMA Director Brown and Department of Homeland Security Director Michael Chertoff become aware of the situation at the convention center.

September 2: At 8 A.M., National Guard troops arrive at the Superdome and the convention center to provide security and begin evacuations to shelters in other parts of the country.

September 12: Michael Brown resigns.

2006 The World Meteorological Organization retires the name Katrina.

2007 A report from the American Society of Civil Engineers concludes that design flaws are to blame for the failure of New Orleans levees. Efforts to rebuild areas affected by Hurricane Katrina are still underway.

Glossary

Coriolis effect A physical phenomenon that explains why winds in Northern Hemisphere storms rotate counterclockwise and winds in the Southern Hemisphere rotate clockwise. Both are due to Earth's rotation.

cyclone A weather pattern in which air masses rapidly circulate inward toward a low-pressure center and are typically accompanied by severe rains. Cyclones circulate counterclockwise in the Northern Hemisphere and clockwise in the Southern Hemisphere.

Federal Emergency Management Agency Also known as FEMA, this is a federal agency that falls under the jurisdiction of the Department of Homeland Security and is responsible for coordinating federal disaster preparation and response.

hurricane A tropical cyclone that originates near the equator in the Atlantic Ocean, Caribbean Sea, or eastern regions of the Pacific Ocean and brings heavy rains and winds in excess of 72 miles per hour.

levee An embankment constructed along a river in order to prevent flooding.

National Hurricane Center A federal agency, located in Miami, Florida, that is responsible for predicting and monitoring tropical depressions, tropical storms, and hurricanes.

parish An area of political jurisdiction in Louisiana that is equivalent to what other states refer to as counties.

Saffir-Simpson Hurricane Scale A scale that assigns hurricanes a rating of 1–5, based on wind speeds, as a measure of their intensity

storm surge A flood of ocean or lake water that occurs during tropical storms or hurricanes.

tropical storm A tropical cyclone in which wind speed is constant and averages 39–73 miles per hour.

United States Army Corps of Engineers A military organization composed of 34,600 civilian and 650 enlisted men and women that builds military facilities, dams, levees, and other civil engineering projects.

wetlands Lands where soil is saturated with water; they are important buffers to hurricanes.

Bibliography

"51 New Orleans Police Employees Fired." Associated Press. Available online. URL: http://www.usatoday.com/news/nation/2005-10-28-copsfired_x.htm. Updated October 29, 2005.

"Aftermath of Hurricane Katrina." *CNN: The Situation Room.* Available online. URL: http://transcripts.cnn.com/TRANSCRIPTS/0509/01/sitroom.02.html. September 1, 2005.

"*American Morning*: Transcript," CNN. Available online. URL: http://transcripts.cnn.com/TRANSCRIPTS/0509/02/ltm.01.html. September 2, 2005.

Anderson, Ed, and Jan Moller. "Looting Difficult to Control." *New Orleans Times-Picayune.* Available online. URL: http://www.nola.com/newslogs/breakingtp/index.ssf?/ mtlogs/nola_Times-Picayune/archives/2005_08.html. August 31, 2005.

Barbaro, Michael, and Justin Gillis. "Wal-Mart at Forefront of Hurricane Relief." *Washington Post.* Available online. URL: http://www.washingtonpost.com/wp-dyn/content/article/2005/09/05/AR2005090501598.html. September 6, 2005.

Berger, Eric. "Keeping Its Head Above Water." *Houston Chronicle.* Available online. URL: http://hurricane.lsu.edu/_in_the_news/houston.htm. December 1, 2001.

Brinkley, Douglas. *The Great Deluge.* New York: Morrow, 2006.

Brooks, Karen. "Worst Thing I've Ever Seen." *Dallas Morning News.* Available online. URL: http://www.dallasnews.com/sharedcontent/dws/news/katrina/stories/ 090805dntexkatrita.2ee8c38.html. September 8, 2005.

Brooks, Karen, and Pete Slover. "911 Calls During Catastrophe Ranged from Calm to Panic to Death." *Dallas Morning News.* September 14, 2005.

Bumiller, Elisabeth. "Casualty of Firestorm: Outrage, Bush and FEMA Chief." *New York Times.* Available online. URL: http://www.nytimes.com/2005/09/10/national/nationalspecial/

10crisis.html?ex=1284004800&en=5bad978de166d894&ei=5090&partner=rssuserland&emc=rss. September 10, 2005.

Calder, Chad. "Gun Sales Surge Still Going Strong." *Advocate*. September 15, 2005.

"Climate of 2005 Atlantic Hurricane Season." National Climatic Data Center. Available online. URL: http://www.ncdc.noaa.gov/oa/climate/research/2005/hurricanes05.html

Cohen, Adam. "Editorial Observer; If the Big One Hits the Big Easy, the Good Times May Be over Forever." *New York Times*. August 11, 2002.

Connolly, Ceci. "Thousands of 911 Katrina Calls Went Astray." *Washington Post*. Available online. URL: http://www.washingtonpost.com/wp-dyn/content/article/2005/11/07/AR2005110701334.html. November 8, 2005.

Coviello, Will. "Last Call: One Man's Odyssey out of New Orleans." *Independent Weekly*. Available online. URL: http://www.indyweek.com/gyrobase/PrintFriendly? oid=oid%3A25122. September 7, 2005.

Davis, Mike, and Anthony Fontenot. "Hurricane Gumbo." *Nation*. Available online. URL: http://www.thenation.com/doc/20051107/davis/2. Updated October 20, 2005.

"Design Shortcomings Seen in New Orleans Flood Walls." *New York Times*. Available online. URL: http://www.nytimes.com/2005/09/21/national/nationalspecial/21walls.html ?ex=1284955200&en=d4b9306b8d5dde06&ei=5088&partner=rssnyt&emc=rss. Updated September 12, 2005.

Duffy, Brian. "Anatomy of a Disaster: 5 Days That Changed a Nation." *U.S. News and World Report*. Available online. URL: http://www.usnews.com/usnews/news/articles/050926/26saturday.htm. September 26, 2005.

Dwyer, Jim, and Christopher Drew. "Fear Exceeded Crime's Reality in New Orleans." *New York Times*. Available online. URL: http://www.nytimes.com/2005/09/29/national/nationalspecial/29crime.html?ei=5090&en=1ba20914f5888e1

0&ex=1285646400&partner=rssuserland&emc=rss&pagewanted=print. September 29, 2005.

Dyson, Michael Eric. *Come Hell or High Water.* New York: Basic Civitas, 2006.

"Ebbert Expects Casualties." *New Orleans Times-Picayune.* Available online. URL: http://nola.live.advance.net/weblogs/print.ssf?/mtlogs/nola_Times-Picayune/archives/ print074900.html.

"Fats Domino Found OK in New Orleans." CNN. Available online. URL: http://www.cnn.com/2005/SHOWBIZ/Music/09/01/katrina.fats.domino/index.html. September 1, 2005.

"FEMA Chief Taken off On-Site Efforts." FOXNews.com. Available online. URL: http://www.foxnews.com/story/0,2933,168915,00.html. September 10, 2005.

Fisher, Marc. "Essential Again." *American Journalism Review.* Available online. URL: http://www.ajr.org/Article.asp?id=3962. October/November 2005.

Foster, Mary. "Hurricane Katrina Rips Superdome Roof." Associated Press. Available online. URL: http://www.sfgate.com/cgi-bin/article.cgi?f=/n/a/2005/08/29/national/a163816D53.DTL. August 30, 2005.

Giles, Nancy. "What if they were white?" *CBS News Sunday Morning.* Available online. URL: http://www.cbsnews.com/stories/2005/09/04/sunday/main814720.shtml

Gilgoff, Dan. "Big Blow in the Big Easy." *U.S. News and World Report.* Available online. URL: http://www.usnews.com/usnews/news/articles/050718/18neworleans.htm

Good Morning America. ABC News. September 1, 2005.

"Grandma's Sausage Looting Charge Dismissed." Associated Press. Available online. URL: http://www.msnbc.msn.com/id/10837203/from/RSS/. Updated January 13, 2006.

Griggs, Susan. "Despite Stormy Start, Katrina Baby Thrives." Air Force Link: The Official Web Site of the United States Air Force. Available online. URL: http://www.af.mil/news/story.asp?id=123022656. July 1, 2006.

Grissett, Sheila. "Frustration, Anger Grown in Jeff over Removal of Pump Operators." *New Orleans Times-Picayune*. Available online. URL: http://www.nola.com/newslogs/breakingtp/index.ssf?/mtlogs/nola_Times-Picayune/archives/2005_10_06.html. October 6, 2005.

Grunwald, Michael. "State Leads in Army Corps Spending, but Millions Had Nothing to Do with Floods." *Washington Post*. Available online. URL: http://www.washingtonpost.com/wp-dyn/content/article/2005/09/07/ AR2005090702462.html. September 8, 2005.

Hannity and Colmes. Fox News. September 2, 2005.

Heidorn, Keith C. "Louisiana's Great Hurricane of 1722." Island.net. Available online. URL: http://www.islandnet.com/~see/weather/events/lahurr1722.htm

"How Hurricanes Form and Die." *Enchanted Learning*. Available online. URL: http://www.enchantedlearning.com/subjects/weather/hurricane/formation.shtml

"How New Orleans Flooded." Nova Science Programming On Air and Online. Available online. URL: http://www.pbs.org/wgbh/nova/orleans/how-nf.html

"In Case of Emergency," *New Orleans Times-Picayune*. Available online. URL: http://www.ohsep.louisiana.gov/newsrelated/incaseofemrgencyexercise.htm. July 20, 2004.

"Katrina: One Man's Search." BBC News. Available online. URL: http://news.bbc.co.uk/nolavconsole/ukfs_news/hi/newsid_4560000/newsid_4562500/bb_wm_4562532.stm.

"Katrina's Animal Rescue." PBS. Available online. URL: http://www.pbs.org/wnet/nature/katrina.

Kestenbaum, David. "Why Did the 17th Street Canal Levee Fail?" National Public Radio. Available online. URL: http://www.npr.org/templates/story/story.php?storyId=5418521. May 19, 2006.

Krugman, Paul. "A Can't-Do Government," *New York Times*. Available online. URL: http://www.nytimes.com/2005/09/02/

opinion/02krugman.html?ex=1283313600&en=3bad12fcbf7ee0ae&ei=5090&partner=rssuserland&emc=rs. Updated September 2, 2005.

Lee, Spike. "When the Levees Broke: A Requiem in Four Acts." HBO Home Video, 2006.

Louisiana Gator Boys. "New Orleans." *Blues Brothers 2000:* Music Soundtrack. Universal, 1998.

Manjoo, Farhad, Page Rockwell, and Aaron Kinney "Timeline to Disaster." Salon.com. Available online. URL: http://dir.salon.com/story/news/feature/2005/09/15/ katrina_timeline/index.html. September 15, 2005.

"Mayor to Feds: 'Get off Your Asses.'" CNN. Available online. URL: http://edition.cnn.com/2005/US/09/02/nagin.transcript. September 2, 2005.

"Mississippi Coast Areas Wiped Out." CBSNews.com. Available online. URL: http://www.cbsnews.com/stories/2005/09/01/katrina/main810916.shtml. September 1, 2005.

"New Orleans Braces for the Big One." CNN. Available online. URL: http://www.cnn.com/2005/WEATHER/08/28/katrina.neworleans/index.html - 48k -. August 28, 2005.

"New Orleans: History." City-Data.com. Available online. URL: http://www.city-data.com/us-cities/The-South/New-Orleans-History.html.

"New Orleans Hospital Deaths Still Stump Coroner." CNN. Available online. URL: http://www.cnn.com/2007/LAW/02/01/katrina.hospital/index.html. February 2, 2007.

"New Orleans Police Probe Police Role in Shooting." Associated Press. Available online. URL: http://www.msnbc.msn.com/id/9535751. Updated September 29, 2005.

"No charges for doctor in Katrina hospital deaths." CNN. Available online. URL: http://www.cnn.com/2007/US/law/07/24/katrina.doctor.ap/index.html

Nolan, Bruce. "Katrina Takes Aim." *New Orleans Times-Picayune.* August 28, 2005.

Nossiter, Adam. "Fearful New Orleans Awaits the Dawn of Hurricane Katrina." Associated Press. Available online. URL: http://www.post-gazette.com/pg/05241/561982.stm. August 29, 2005.

Nossiter, Adam. "In Rare Public N.O. Appearance, Morial Brushes Aside Questions." The Associated Press State and Local Wire. August 27, 2005.

Nossiter, Adam. "Rescue Boats in La. Search for Survivors." Associated Press. Available online. URL: http://www.sfgate.com/cgi-bin/article.cgi?f=/n/a/2005/08/30/national/a150730D13.DTL. August 30, 2005.

Olsen, Lise. "City Had Evacuation Plan but Strayed from Strategy." *Houston Chronicle*. September 8, 2005.

"Pledges U.S. Disaster Aid to Louisiana." *Chicago Tribune*. September 10, 1965.

"President Discusses Hurricane Relief in Address to the Nation." White House Press Release. Available online. URL: http://www.whitehouse.gov/news/releases/2005/09/20050915-8.html. September 15, 2005.

Rhoads, Christopher. "After Katrina, City Officials Struggled to Keep Order." *Wall Street Journal*. Available online. URL: http://www.post-gazette.com/pg/05252/ 568686.stm. September 9, 2005.

Riley, John. "Spared from Catastrophe." *Newsday*. Available online. URL: http://www.newsday.com/mynews/ny-usnola304403795aug30,0,2996037.story. August 30, 2005.

Roberts, Michelle. "Families Say Stress of Katrina Hastened Deaths of Loved Ones." Associated Press. Available online. URL: http://www.boston.com/news/nation/articles/2006/12/14/families_say_stress_of_katrina_hastened_deaths_of_loved_ones. December 14, 2006.

Roberts, Penny Brown. "Survivor: 'We Just Couldn't Get Out.'" *Advocate*. August 31, 2005.

"RTA Buses Would Be Used for Evacuation; But Plan Still Falls Short of Needs." *New Orleans Times-Picayune*. July 8, 2005.

Russell, Gordon. "Refugees Find Dome an Intolerable Refuge." *New Orleans Times-Picayune*. September 1, 2005.

Serrano, Richard A. and Nicole Gauoette. "Despite Warnings, Washington Failed to Fund Levee Projects." *The Los Angeles Times*. Available online. URL: http://www.truthout.org/docs_2005/printer_090405B.shtml

Spera, Keith. "Desperation, Death on Road to Safety." *New Orleans Times-Picayune*. Available online. URL: http://www.nola.com/weblogs/print.ssf?/mtlogs/nola_Times-Picayune/archives/print075561.html. August 31, 2005.

"Staff at New Orleans Hospital Debated Euthanizing Patients." CNN. Available online. URL: http://www.cnn.com/2005/US/10/12/katrina.hospital/index.html. October 13, 2005.

"Storm Toll over 50; Damage in Millions." *Los Angeles Times*. September 12, 1965.

"Take Care of the Kids and Grandkids." CNN. Available online. URL: http://www.cnn.com/2005/WEATHER/08/30/katrina.people/index.html. August 30, 2005.

"Testimony of Warren J. Riley, Superintendent of the New Orleans Police Department before the Committee on Homeland Security and Government Affairs." Available online. URL: http://hsgac.senate.gov/_files/020606Riley.pdf. February 6, 2006.

Thibodeaux, Darryl. "New Orleans: Survivor Stories. Cory Delany." Minneapolis/St. Paul *City Pages*. Available online. URL: http://citypages.com/databank/26/1294/ article13694.asp?page=8. September 20, 2005.

"Thousands Remain in Superdome." CBS News. Available online. URL: http://www.cbsnews.com/stories/2005/08/29/national/main799251.shtml?CMP=OTC-RSSFeed&source=RSS&attr=HOME_799251. August 29, 2005.

"Transcripts, Tape Show Bush, Brown Warned on Katrina." CNN. Available online. URL: http://www.cnn.com/2006/POLITICS/03/02/fema.tapes/index.html. March 2, 2006.

Treaster, Joseph. "Superdome: Haven Quickly Becomes an Ordeal." *New York Times*. Available online. URL: http://www.nytimes.com/2005/09/01/national/nationalspecial/01dome.html?ex=1283227200&en=1ab66b38acc69641&ei=5088&partner=rssnyt. September 1, 2005.

Treaster, Joseph, and Kate Zernike. "Katrina Misses New Orleans, Heavily Damages Mississippi." *New York Times*. August 30, 2005.

Williams, Brian. "We Were Witnesses." MSNBC. Available online. URL: http://www.msnbc.msn.com/id/14518359. August 28, 2006.

Wilson, Jamie. "For many, misery starts in Katrina's wake." *The Guardian*. Available online. URL: http://www.guardian.co.uk/katrina/story/0,,1560778,00.html

"Witnesses: New Orleans Cops Took Rolex Watches, Jewelry." CNN. Available online. URL: http://www.cnn.com/2005/US/09/30/nopd.looting/index.html. September 30, 2005.

"Worldwide Tropical Cyclone Names." National Hurricane Center. Available online. URL: http://www.nhc.noaa.gov/aboutnames.shtml. Updated on March 23, 2007.

Zorn, Eric. "'Refugees' vs. 'Evacuees'—The Distinctions and the Difference." Change of Subject: A Chicago Tribune Web Log. Available online. URL: http://blogs.chicago tribune.com/news_columnists_ezorn/2005/09/refugees_vs_eva.html. September 5, 2005.

Zura, James A. "My Welcome to the Tropics." JimZura.com. Available online. URL: http://www.jimzura.com/Update901/PhotoAliciaNotesPage.htm.

Further Reading

Brinkley, Douglas. *The Great Deluge*. New York: Morrow, 2006.

Cooper, Anderson. *Dispatches from the Edge: A Memoir of War, Disasters and Survival*. New York: HarperCollins, 2006.

Dyson, Michael Eric. *Come Hell or High Water*. New York: Basic Civitas, 2006.

Horne, Jed. *Breach of Faith: Hurricane Katrina and the Near Death of a Great American City*. New York: Random House, 2006.

McQuaid, John, and Mark Schleifstein. *Path of Destruction: The Devastation of New Orleans and the Coming Age of Superstorms*. New York : Little, Brown, 2006.

Piazza, Tom. *Why New Orleans Matters*. New York: ReganBooks, 2005.

Rose, Chris. *1 Dead in Attic*. New Orleans: Chris Rose Books, 2005.

Time Magazine, Editors. *Hurricane Katrina: The Storm That Changed America*. New York: Times Books, 2005.

Times-Picayune, The. *Katrina: The Ruin and Recovery of New Orleans*. Champaign, Ill.: Spotlight Press, 2006.

Van Heerden, Ivor, and Mike Bryan. *The Storm: What Went Wrong and Why During Hurricane Katrina*. New York: Viking, 2006.

Picture Credits

8: AP Images, David J. Phillip
13: SMGraphics
15: AP Images, Pat Semansky
18: AP Images, Christine Gerber
24: AP Images
27: AP Images
31: © Smiley N. Pool/Dallas Morning News/Corbis
36: AP Images, Cheryl Gerber
41: AP Images, John Rowland
45: AP Images, Dave Martin
50: AP Images, David J. Phillip
54: AP Images, Eric Gay
59: AP Images, David J. Phillip
64: AP Images, Melissa Phillip
68: AFP/Getty Images
71: AP Images, Bill Haber
76: AFP/Getty Images
83: © Michael Ainsworth/Dallas Morning News/Corbis
89: AP Images, Patrick Dennis
93: AP Images, Brian Cleary
95: AP Images, L.M. Otero
101: AP Images, Joshua Lott
102: AP Images, Alex Brandon
104: AP Images, Alex Brandon
Cover: AP Images

Index

About the Author

JAMIE PIETRAS is a writer and journalist who lives in New York City. He holds an MFA in Creative Writing with a concentration in nonfiction from Columbia University.